About the author

Sonia Neale is the author of *The Bad Mother's Revenge* (ABC Books). She also writes a column for *My Child* magazine and broadcasts regularly on ABC Local Radio, Perth.

Death by Teenager

Death By Teenager

One mum's hilarious account of raising adolescents

Sonia Neale

ABC Books

Published by ABC Books for the
AUSTRALIAN BROADCASTING CORPORATION
GPO Box 9994 Sydney NSW 2001

Copyright © Sonia Neale 2009

First published in April 2009

All rights reserved. No part of this publication may be
reproduced, stored in a retrieval system or transmitted in any
form or by any means, electronic, mechanical, photocopying,
recording or otherwise, without the prior written permission
of the Australian Broadcasting Corporation.

The National Library of Australia Cataloguing-in-Publication entry

Neale, Sonia,
Death by teenager/Sonia Neale.

ISBN 978 0 7333 2418 5 (pbk.)

Adolescence.
Parent and teenager – Humor.
Parenting – Humor.
Australian Broadcasting Corporation.

649.125

Cover by Luke Causby, Blue Cork Design
Typeset in 11 on 16pt Bembo by Kirby Jones

Contents

INTRODUCTION

• xi •

Chapter 1

Q. Are your teenagers all sexed up with nowhere to go?
A. IT'S ALWAYS A GOOD IDEA TO PUT A CONDOM IN YOUR TEENAGER'S SCHOOL LUNCHBOX.

• 1 •

Chapter 2

Q. Is fast food in the faster lane making you giddy?
A. WHEN YOU EAT AT THE FAMILY DINING TABLE, IT'S ALWAYS PRUDENT TO USE PLASTIC CUTLERY.

• 21 •

Chapter 3

Q. Should children clean their bedroom before saving the planet?
A. EVEN AL GORE HID CRUSTY UNDERWEAR AND MILK-FILLED CEREAL BOWLS UNDER THE BED.

• 41 •

Chapter 4

Q. Why is it easier to Facebook than to get your teen's face in a book?
A. IT'S HARD WORK EDUCATING THE INDIFFERENT TO MAKE A DIFFERENCE.

• 59 •

Chapter 5

Q. How do you survive your family?
A. FOLLOW THE IDIOT'S GUIDE TO THE STOCKHOLM SYNDROME.

• 79 •

Chapter 6

Q. Shrink-wrapped on the other side of the couch and wondering who to blame?
A. MUST BE YOUR MOTHER, YOUR THERAPIST ... OR YOURSELF.

• 103 •

Chapter 7

Q. Waves of emotions or tsunamis of guilt?
A. EMO IS NOT A DIRTY WORD.

• 125 •

Chapter 8

Q. Want a nostalgia trip?
A. TURN OFF THE COMPUTER AND OPEN A WINDOW.

• 145 •

Chapter 9

Q. What do flatulence, bloodsucking creatures and teenagers have in common?
A. THEY'RE REALLY AWFUL THINGS THAT NEED TO BE REPRESSED IMMEDIATELY.

• 165 •

Chapter 10

Q. Why do I kiss my son while twisting his earlobes?
A. JUST ONE OF THE MANY WAYS TO EXPRESS MOTHER LOVE.

• 181 •

ACKNOWLEDGMENTS

• 203 •

Introduction

Remember the National Lampoon movie *Vacation* with Chevy Chase, about the Griswold family bumbling their way towards Walley World? We are that family, only with the added bonus of a few anger management issues.

It's a teenager's duty to be rude, angry and rebellious and it's a parent's job to guide that rudeness, anger and rebellion into acceptable social behaviour, without feeling the need to chase them around the room with the sharp edge of the gladwrap. I love my teenagers but there are times when I don't like them. Sometimes the only time we don't get cross with each other is when they are asleep and I'm sitting down writing about them and I experience a rush of tenderness I don't necessarily feel around about 3.30pm each weekday when they come barging through the front door, hungry and irritable after yet another boringly BORING day at school.

There are no thick, glossy magazines called *My Beautiful Teenager*, showing a proud, glowing mother cradling a couch-bound, well-fed, raggedy-jean-clad adolescent sleeping like a baby, surrounded by pizza crusts with a teat-covered coke bottle firmly wedged between their lips. No-one says, 'Congratulations! It's a teenager' when they turn thirteen.

Yet...

When they're not throwing poison darts at me, my teenagers can be my best friends. Let me introduce them to you. My younger son, Christopher, the SmartRider, can work out Fibonacci sequences and explain Pythagoras's theorem in his sleep. He gets intimately tied up in quantum string theory and can make his own Mobius strip. However he gets flummoxed when working out how many cylinders a V8 Commodore has.

My elder son Matthew, the Dreamer, not only knows how many cylinders a V8 engine has, he knows how and why they work in sequence and he can build a Franken-scooter out of a pair of old bike tyres, some corrugated iron and a lawn-mower engine, but thinks a Mobius strip is a form of pornographic dancing.

But they also have a lot in common. They both burp rude comments and fart prolifically at the dinner table, wear their jeans commando-style, half-mast, while continuously bending over to pick up imaginary fluff off the floor for the benefit of their harassed mother, and can spend up to 3 hours in a locked bathroom under the shower without even getting wet. They can shoot a basketball hoop from 20 metres but cannot aim directly into the toilet bowl. Nor can they get themselves ready for school without revving their parents up into a frenzied fury.

My daughter, Melissa, the Wild Child, plays complicated guitar riffs, reads heavy psychological books and consults Wikipedia the way most people check their watches. She works as a gourmet chef but is addicted to Subway and Maccas. She is talking of leaving home to travel the world and one of my hands is pushing her firmly out the door and the other one is hugging her tightly.

I enjoy their company but if I ever want to clear the lounge room I light my scented candles and play my favourite meditation CD or *The Bee Gee's Greatest Hits*. They can't leave fast enough and it works without fail every time: an instant teenager-free zone.

I need this space because parenting isn't what I thought it would be. I thought if I loved my kids enough they would never misbehave and I used to take motherhood very seriously — until I actually gave birth.

After which I became serious about communicating with my children in a way they could all understand. While many eons ago my parents lectured me and my sister in person, computers have taken over our household and it's easier to global email or text my children to clean their rooms and pick up their smelly clothes than it is to bend their ears in person. Or if there's an interesting piece of news on the internet I send it to them for dinner table discussion that night. Especially now I have time on my hands.

I gave up full-time work recently, much to the dismay of the SmartRider and the Dreamer. When I cook their breakfast, make their lunch and remind them to do their homework, they just groan and want me to go back to work and stop caring and sharing so much because it gets on their nerves. So much for the sorrows of latch-key kids. They love their personal space; besides, it's difficult to surf for porn when your mother is breathing down your neck. One time I went up and gave the Dreamer a hug from behind when he was on the computer and he said, "Mum, I'm on *the webcam*". Vintage stuff. It's good to keep them on their toes.

Parenting is the most important job in the world. With all its bitter sweetness, it's the most satisfying and rewarding journey

I've ever undertaken. Sometimes family life is not pretty, but it seems to turn out OK in the end. There are psychic ties that bind all of us to our families, because no one will ever love us in quite the same way they do.

1

Q. Are your teenagers all sexed up with nowhere to go?

A. IT'S ALWAYS A GOOD IDEA TO PUT A CONDOM IN YOUR TEENAGER'S SCHOOL LUNCHBOX.

It's all about sex, baby

My two boys, the Dreamer and the SmartRider, went to Sydney to stay with my sister during the recent Christmas holidays. But it wasn't the Opera House, the Harbour Bridge, or even the Powerhouse Museum that was the highlight of their trip. It was checking out the bronzed, bare-breasted birds on Bondi Beach.

So, what do you do when your children become more interested in 'willies', 'frontbottoms' and 'bazookas' than they are in Butt Ugly Martians and Power Rangers? That's right, you botch it up as you did the rest of your parenting career, the same way your parents did when they, hand-grenade style, lobbed a *So, You're About to Become a Teenager* book through your bedroom door before beating a hasty retreat and covering their ears.

But when the horny hormonals hit the home front, the best thing to do is, well, simply get used to it. Like Gordon Ramsay's ever-increasing mistress count and indiscretions by leading Australian sportsmen, it's not going to disappear in a hurry.

'It's all about SEX, Mum,' my two boys say as they pelvic-thrust their way around the room to the Black Eyed Peas singing 'My Humps. My Humps. My Lovely Little Lumps'. I get the impression this song has absolutely nothing to do with a camel.

And then, as I breathe rapidly in and out of a paper bag, I'm reminded of yet another of the joys of parenting — when you find your gorgeous primary-school darlings playing doctors and nurses. In my case, while the children themselves went on happily to live another day, I needed yet more therapy. And then, aside from finding your kids indulging in an act that can best be described as *ER Meets Debbie Does Dallas*, finding porn hidden under your teenager's mattress is enough to give you a cardiac arrest. But sometimes it's not you finding covert stashes in your children's bedroom that's the problem, it's them discovering the unexpected in yours.

Many years ago, the SmartRider and I were doing a school project that required a pair of scissors. I told him to look in the drawer, meaning the desk drawer. He went to my bedside drawer instead and held up what was definitely NOT a pair of scissors (actually it was a bedroom power tool) and asked me what it was. After I unclawed myself from the ceiling, I informed him that it was 'something that didn't cut paper'.

Teen shriek

EMOSHUN
Angst-ridden children who think and feel deeply, and are therefore taunted and shunned by non-depressed children.

TRAUMA-TIES
The process that binds you psychically to your mother and father, brothers and sisters, and any other relatives who get on your nerves.

PRETTY IN PUNK
An oxymoron: punk is anything but rosy and attractive.

PAIR-RENTALS
The pair who gave birth to His or Her Royal Highness. The term derives from the rent he or she refuses to pay to them for the living space occupied after he or she gets his/her first full-time job.

RE-BELLY-ION
Piercing one's belly-button (and other, more unmentionable, body parts) several times in order to send a message to your pair-rentals and the rest of the world that you really are cool, independent and not influenced by the rest of the crowd.

ADDLEDESCENCE
The time that hormones addle the pubescent boy-brain into thinking it's an excellent idea to photocopy one's backside just as the deputy principal is walking through the door. An extreme example is thinking this when you are the head boy of your primary school.

PIM-PULLS
The compelling psychic urge to squeeze and torture facial blemishes till they spurt lava-like over the bathroom mirror. This is best captured by being snapped on a mobile phone and then uploaded onto YouTube, where 'squeezing pimples' can be typed into a search engine.

ACNE-CYCLE
The bike ridden to school in order to get fresh air, sunshine and exercise to try to clear those awful facial blemishes that are the bane of a teenager's existence. Failing that, it's the vehicle that gets him or her to the chemist for some pim-pull cream.

ALIEN ABDUCTION
Something that happens around about puberty, when your darling, level-headed, compliant child gets abducted, virtually overnight, by alien spaceships and replaced by a moody, angst-ridden, pim-pully, rebellious teenager.

TEST-OSTERONE
When your oldest son continually tests your husband's patience with grandstanding displays of overt aggression that generally involve a spinning wet tea towel whipped ferociously against naked flesh that is usually, but not necessarily, his younger brother's.

ANGST-RIDDEN
Not unlike the acne-cycle, this is the bike ride the teenager takes when feeling especially sorry for him or herself after a tragic argument with overbearing pair-rentals.

HOME-WORK
Something to be avoided at all costs, lest some global knowledge be gained that may benefit him or her in the future.

VOICE-BREAKING
What happens when Mother has spent her time and energy screaming at the top of her lungs at her lazy children to tidy up their bedrooms until both she and her voice break down and cry.

CON-DOMS
Thin bits of Glad Wrap most teenagers get scammed into thinking will prevent STDs, underage pregnancy and the potential emotional devastation of their first sexual encounter.

SEX-DRIVE
The distance teenagers will go in their cars to find a safe place to have unsafe sex.

SEXUAL URGES
When your parents desperately urge you not to have sex till you are at least 35, earn over $100,000 and own your own house, car, speed boat and share portfolio.

MEN-STRUATION
Something the male of the species never has to suffer unless he's married, or has a mother or a girlfriend, or, if he's really lucky, all three.

GENERATION X-TRA
The group of people born around about 1960 who always give that extra little bit and have learned the hard way that working for a living involves giving everything one has in order to receive not only personal satisfaction but a reasonably good income.

GENERATION-WHINY-ARSE
The newest and youngest worker, born around 1985, who thinks filing and photocopying is beneath him or her. However, if he or she does have to do it, he or she should be paid an executive-level salary and have numerous fringe benefits and a corner window office with a tenth-storey view, as well as a company car (usually a Jaguar or a Mercedes-Benz) complete with chauffeur, DVD player and well-stocked bar fridge.

The games we play

I had to punish my younger son the other day for continually being rude to his father. Seeing as how a good whack to the back of the head is now considered politically, socially, psychologically and morally incorrect, I decided instead to cut off both his oxygen supply and reason for living — by disconnecting the computer modem and taking it to work with me.

My kids only have two states of mind: vegging out with endless, mindless, computer games and MSN or experiencing unadulterated, mind-numbing boredom. In my day, BCR (not Bay City Rollers but Before Computers Ruled) we had something called The Great Outdoors, where, as a child I used to disappear from dawn till dusk during the summer holidays. When stuck indoors during the winter ones, board games ruled and Monopoly was King.

Mum ALWAYS used to let me win in my childhood, because if I didn't win EVERY time I was an insufferable little gobshite. (So, apparently I was a bad loser but, as I've always told her, I made up for it by being a good winner.) And there I was thinking I was an expert on, and champion of, the game. My kids tell me board games are called board games because they are — well, boring. I tell my kids that sometimes they have to be — well, bored.

So, despite suffering the pangs of virtual-reality withdrawal, my husband and I decided that in order to punish our rude son we would all go computer-less for a couple of days. United we stand, and divided we actually got some work done around the house.

Not only did a creative meal get cooked and some long-neglected homework get finished, but out of the bowels of the cupboard came the dusty, moth-eaten Monopoly game — and the battle lines were immediately drawn. Rude son immediately declared himself the banker (not that he's a control freak or anything) while I poured myself a large glass of tolerance and understanding. By the pure grace of God, I landed on Park Lane and Mayfair in the first two rounds and bought two hotels, and ten minutes later the game was over and I was bouncing around the room with glee, which goes to prove that I am NOT my mother after all.

So, while it might NOT be in anyone's best interests to give my son a good clip round the ear, there ARE plenty of other, legal, ways to give him a well-deserved thrashing.

The truth about dogs and dogs

If there's a truth about cats and dogs, there's also a truth about dogs and dogs. That is, while all fluffy little terriers and Saint Bernards are created equally, and may even have the same mother and father and be raised in the same dysfunctional households, that will sometimes be where the similarities end.

The best way to explain the differences between my two boys would be telling you two of the movies I've taken them to. One wanted to see *An Inconvenient Truth* and the other wanted to see *Snakes on a Plane*. When it comes to hobbies, one goes out to the bush to paintball while the other is happy to sit at home reading *Vegetarianism for Buddhists*.

However, when I ask them to do their homework, feed the animals, set the table or empty the dishwasher, it's united we stand, divided we fall. Bonded in brotherly love against the common enemy — their parents.

The differences continue when it comes to preferred modes of transport. One rollerblades and rides his bike around the universe, and the other wants to buy a V8 Commodore for his next birthday. (This is not so different from my husband, who recently purchased his latest mid-life crisis in the shape of a blood-red 4WD.)

Women going through the change of life tend to veer towards small, grey, environmentally friendly cars, whereas most blokes seem to think the bigger the car, the better the drive and the larger the experience. Size does matter, which also translates when it comes to barbecuing. My husband enjoys a huge T-bone steak, whereas I prefer a small beef fillet.

Over the years, I've learned not to get in the way when my husband regresses into a Neanderthal excitedly discovering the mysteries of fire every time he lights up the portable gas barbecue. Like sheds and garages, it's a caveman thing. Why do men want to build a BBQ kitchen in the back garden whereas we women look at it as just something else to clean?

The Dreamer turned into a man two years ago. For his thirteenth birthday, we set up the tent in the back garden and lit a campfire big enough to be seen from outer space. Both boys and their mates barbecued to their hearts' content, with eggplant and zucchini sitting side by side in harmony with snaggers and chops.

Later that evening in the tent, they conducted primitive initiation ceremonies and rituals that involved PlayStations, Nintendo DSs, wedgies and marshmallows. That is, secret boys-to-men stuff that we girls, and mothers, pretend not to know about.

It's not about the bike, the barby, or the blood-red 4WD. It's all about being Top Dog and who can bark the loudest.

The bra boys

Going shopping with his mother is a bittersweet experience for my younger boy the SmartRider. I might be buying him a new DS game but first we're just going to pop into Myer because I need some bras 'n' things.

Parental underwear, like birthday present thank-you phone calls, table manners, tofu hamburgers and tampon adverts, is something no teenage boy-brain ever wants to visit, and accompanying his mother on an underwear shopping spree can sometimes require intense debriefing and post-traumatic-stress therapy.

The agony is in seeing his tracky-crack-dacked, middle-aged, saggy-baggy mother standing by the check-out counter in front of two very hot teenage girls, with three pairs of nude-coloured 42DDs and matching Bridget Jones big underpants clutched in her wrinkled, liver-spotted, gnarled hands. The ecstasy is glimpsing, via peripheral vision, the skimpily-clad, g-stringed, extremely adolescent mannequins with pieces of pink dental floss covering their bare bosoms, even if this triggers off strange hormonal feelings he'd rather not be feeling — especially in public and especially with his mother present. (Sometimes there's more in-your-face porn at Myer's lingerie department than can be filtered through the NannyNet on the computer.)

Furthermore, no teenage boy wants to see his mother's knickers nestled against his Bugs Bunny boxers in the family washing basket. When I ask my boys to sort out their socks and jocks from my grey desperadoes, they use a pair of tongs just in case their hands come in contact with something that once covered my Great Southern Land. Of course, touching said items with their bare hands would necessitate either sterilising them with bleach, immersing them in boiling oil or chopping them off altogether — the latter being the preferable option.

This is not unlike the time their grandfather bought some jocks for himself, and, upon trying them on and discovering they were the wrong size, passed them on to my husband and boys. The unanimous verdict was that they had to go in the rubbish bin. Pronto! And the bin had to be burned.

What makes my children's faces blaze hotter than crimson French knickers and matching suspender belt, is catching their parents walking around the house dressed only in their Reg Grundys. This has the same effect on their eyes as looking directly into the sun.

But sometimes it is completely unavoidable. The odds of sneaking unseen into the laundry to grab your skirt or shirt at 6 am on a Monday are in direct proportion to the amount of ironing you didn't do the night before. Chances are this is the exact time your teenagers stumble in bleary-eyed, making a beeline for the toilet, and run smack-bang into their semi-naked mother.

Still, aside from protecting your early-morning dignity from your sleepy adolescents, underwear serves pretty much the same purpose as a shop-window front. It provides an attractive facade for what lurks beneath.

Sex messages

When I was in first year high school, back in the late seventies, boys were disgusting creatures covered in boy germs. So, I was quarantined off to an all-girls Catholic school where my initiation into sex education was when the nuns pulled down and ripped up a picture of naked *Cleo* centrefold of the month Jack Thompson, and his strategically placed guitar, from the virginal walls of our Year Ten classroom. The entire class got a rap on the knuckles with a metal-edged ruler and a frightfully stern lecture from a blushing nun on the evils not only of good-looking men with phallic-looking instruments but of erupting volcanoes as well.

Thanks to my strict Catholic upbringing, I've thought of nothing but sex since I left school. But, according to a best-selling book called *The Female Brain* by a neuro-psychiatrist based in California, while men think about sex every time they see a woman, women think about sex only once a day.

But I've only got to look at a picture of Daniel Craig, and all thoughts about neatly sewing up the hems of my new net curtains go straight out the window and I'm racing down to the local DVD shop to hire *Casino Royale* for the sole purpose of freeze-framing the moment when James Bond emerges dripping wet from the sea. (It's always a toss-up between that or Arnie Schwarzenegger at the beginning of *The Terminator*.)

This may be why the standards of our household are lower-slung than a pair of teenage boy's jeans with baggy boxers hanging out the top. (This is a ghastly trend the demise of which will only occur when we middle-aged mothers rebel en masse by wearing our Bridget Jones' bloomers on the outside of our Harry High Pants — and loiter enthusiastically against the wall of the local supermarket ogling the sexy senior citizens who shuffle slowly past.)

Another image that makes my children shudder violently is the soul-chilling thought of their mother and father indulging in unbridled parental passion. A friend of theirs recently commented that he hoped beyond hope he was adopted because then there was still the vague chance that his parents had never had sex.

And I hope against hope that our joint parental sex education talks have gotten through to our hormonally challenged children. On more than one occasion, my husband and I have walked into a darkened lounge room only to see two shadowy figures, allegedly watching *Happy Feet*, spring apart like someone threw a bucket of cold water over them.

Verifying varekai

'Varekai' is not just an almost unpronounceable French word that means impossible positions. It's also a mind-blowing experience for those of us who are about as flexible as a rusty ironing board.

Sitting in the fifth row of Cirque du Soleil with my mostly inflexible family, I realised that some performers can bend themselves into more contortions than I could inflict on a Barbie doll with my bare hands during a menopausal mood swing.

One muscular female performer, dressed in a glittery skin-coloured costume, squished herself into a flattened 'C' shape with her pelvic area looking straight towards my two teenage boys. They both turned red and hid their faces behind their hands. I just wondered how and when her liver and spleen would spring back into shape after being squashed flatter than one of the starched and pressed, ironed-to-perfection work shirts my husband requires in order to mentally contort himself at work.

And it's flexibility of the mind, more than of the body, that's required to be the mother of two teenage boys. While I haven't yet found hardcore porn under their mattresses, I have discovered that someone in our household has typed the words 'big, flouncy, bouncy, French, double DD cup breasts' into Google. It wasn't me. It wasn't my husband and it wasn't my eighteen-year-old daughter. But my boys visibly squirmed when I confronted them with the internet evidence.

That's where having a mindset as malleable as a circus gymnast comes in handy. Boys are fascinated with breasts and other female body parts. My husband tells me it's normal, and it doesn't mean they're going to turn into spin bowlers who text message their lovers and accidentally send the missive to their spouse instead.

Pushing them in the direction of sport is a good way to keep teenage boys occupied, but I think we might just have our sons give cricket a miss this season.

Conversations with women

When middle-aged women go out to lunch, you can guarantee the topic of conversation is NOT going to be the most effective way to remove grease stains from their husbands' work clothes. Nor will it be how to entertain bored children on rainy weekends, or how to scrape dried food off a ceiling without falling off the ladder and breaking your ironing arm.

We bored ourselves to death back in the early nineties, slowly sipping instant coffee through tight smiles at play group while we tried to outdo each other by lying through our back teeth about what wonderful mothers of perfect children we were.

Now that we're fat, 40, forgetful, flatulent and work full-time, all we want to talk about is the important stuff, like good books, fabulous wine, Bruce Willis, and wild, wild, wanton sex.

No matter how the conversation might have started at a girls' lunch out, by the time we get to the cafe-latte stage, like a fantasy date with the *Die Hard* star, it always ends up involving sex hotter than our drinks. It's somehow liberating to find out whether anyone else is getting more, less, better, worse, different, more indifferent, exciting or disappointing sex than oneself. And most of my friends don't hold back when it comes to being forward, either.

We're not discussing measurements, statistics, best pick-up lines, or talking about swinging from chandeliers. That's boring beyond belief and best left to the businessmen who frequent the front bars of pubs and hotels.

The talk is more about the absurdities of why we do what we do, how we do it, how we feel about how we do it, and about whether Brad Pitt and Angelina Jolie do it three times a night, or once a fortnight like the rest of us. Some of the best Tupperware parties I've ever been to were those where the conversation centred on the rude and ridiculous rather than overrated, over-priced food containers.

At my age, I'm just not interested in Stepford-wifing the shelves of my pantry with lifetime-guaranteed plastic. I'd rather spend my precious time and money going out to lunch once a week, laughing a lot and raising my glass — and a few eyebrows — to interesting conversation.

So, if you hear hoots of laughter coming from a rollicking table of women at a restaurant, you'll have a pretty good idea of what the conversation is all about. A long, boozy lunch with a group of middle-aged girls is, in itself, sometimes better than sex.

Rottnest rules

Virginia Woolf said that 'every woman needs a room of her own' and, in addition to this wisdom, there's my belief that every woman needs a travelling companion she isn't married to.

Until recently, the last time I stayed at Rottnest was on my honeymoon. Bob Hawke was the Prime Minister, the current crop of West Coast Eagles were still in nappies, Humphrey B Bear was wiggling the under-fives and *Fatal Attraction* was, supposedly, keeping married men on the straight and narrow. After a recent child- and husband-free Rottnest holiday, I discovered that the normal rules of society don't apply on an overseas trip taken with a girlfriend who's a couch-jumping footy fan who could make Gordon Ramsay blush with her choice of language.

While footy fever around grand final time is contagious, it was always something my husband and I seemed actively inoculated against. I had never watched a footy match in its entirety — ever. Call me unAustralian, but when we emigrated from England in 1968 I took to meat pies, kangaroos and Holden cars but not football. The Rottnest Island holiday, though, meant that it wasn't only on Pinky Beach during schoolies week that I lost my virginity, it was also in the Quokka's Arms during the closest football match in AFL history. Thanks to my enthusiastic girlfriend, I briefly became the West Coast Eagles second-most rabid supporter. I was a football slut for the night while still remaining faithful to my rugby-loving husband.

I hadn't realised I was going to be watching football history. I learned a new word that night — Wirrpunda. I also discovered that a magpie isn't just a black-and-white bird that swoops dangerously during spring.

It wasn't just about the game, it was about comradeship and fitting in authentically with a different crowd. I became a true Australian that night, bonding over beer and wine, boofheads and bikes, and blue-and-yellow scarves. Even the quokkas looked genuinely excited.

Had I gone to Rottnest with my husband, we would have avoided the 'F' word altogether and had a quiet drink in our chalet before reading, relaxing and writing predictable postcards to the children. Which just goes to show that breaking out and doing something completely different with a person other than your spouse helps to keep a 20-year-old marriage unpredictable and rather exciting.

He and I still have holidays together but we now also have holidays apart. I don't have a room, or even a computer, to call my own but I do have a travelling companion.

Husbands are great but sometimes going away with girlfriends is better.

Duelling guitars

One Sunday morning not too long ago, I awoke to the sweet sound of duelling guitars — which is a far more pleasant experience than waking up to the sound of duelling siblings.

Mu daughter, the Wild Child is now the proud owner of an electric guitar and amplifier, and has ceremoniously passed her acoustic one down the bloodline to her younger brother. It could have been worse — I have it on the best authority that if your teenager wants to be in a band, never, EVER, be the mother who owns the child who owns the drum kit.

Guitars are portable in a way that drum kits aren't. Wherever the drum kit gets put down, that's its home. And if it's your house, it's time to run away to live in a much quieter place, such as the front row of the Burswood Dome in the middle of an AC/DC concert.

The, non-portable, drum kit attracts to its house all the budding Eric Claptons and Mark Knopflers, as well as their entourage in the shape of beer cans, hand-rolled cigarettes, excruciatingly loud bum guitar notes, grungy emos, angry neighbours, barking dogs and regular visits from the local constabulary. So, when the Wild Child bought an electric guitar in order for her garage band to play at some other mother's house, I was very, very happy indeed.

Teenagers and loud music go together like bored housewives and imaginary romantic encounters in Paris without husbands or musically inclined children. It's an escape from humdrum existence that catapults one from not getting any satisfaction to climbing the stairway to heaven in a single bound.

Now that she's mastered that Led Zeppelin classic, as well as 'Smoke on the Water' and the theme from *SpongeBob SquarePants*, she's expanding her horizons by writing her own music and lyrics. The song I've asked her to play over and over again is 'I've Tidied Up My Bedroom and Paid My Board on Time'!

That's not on her playlist — not even in her Top 100. But the song and dance she's led us over the years has been far more impressive and electrifying than any guitar and amplifier could ever be.

We now just have to educate her on the fact that three o'clock in the morning isn't the best time for a plugged-in session. We also have to inform our other guitarless son that banging on about a drum kit for Christmas is about as likely to get him what he wants as me trekking around Europe without the family.

2

Q. Is fast food in the faster lane making you giddy?

A. WHEN YOU EAT AT THE FAMILY DINING TABLE, IT'S ALWAYS PRUDENT TO USE PLASTIC CUTLERY.

Mutant casserole

As with the deceptively immaculate mansions in Wisteria Lane, most seemingly normal people hug guilty secrets close to their hearts or indulge in cloak-and-dagger behaviour that loudly rattles the skeletons in their sleek, glossy, colour-coordinated closets. Or, as in our case, not so much a skeleton but a huge bloated corpse that buckles and bulges, trying desperately to break free and expose us for what we really are — an ordinary, average, everyday family — at least we appear that way from the outside.

On the inside, the wardrobe skeletons are currently addicted to housework apathy. We don't do the dishes immediately after dinner, we leave them till the following week. Just as disturbing is the drip from the kitchen tap that has now turned into a torrential downpour threatening to flood our suppressed anxiety.

The dancing skeleton in the mosh pit of our pigpen isn't who hogs the phone the most, or who's the most financially irresponsible, or even who ate the last chocolate biscuit, but whose turn it is to scrub out the pot from the burned half-eaten casserole that no-one liked in the first place.

In the war of attrition going on in our household, no-one is willing to take responsibility for such things, and for a week the errant casserole dish got relegated to the too-hard basket and stood on the bench. It was actively ignored, and only investigated when the subsequent humming and buzzing eventually drowned out the sound of *Hell's Kitchen*. Only then did we discover that the contents of the dish contained more mould than the shower floor of the local gym and was as fluorescent as a night club on New Year's Eve.

That was when we decided to throw the baby out with the bathwater, wrapped up the casserole dish in 60 metres of Glad Wrap and, under cover of night, threw it in the wheelie-bin. But this was not before we took video evidence. As we all know, it hasn't happened till it appears on YouTube, in all its time-lapse glory, and thus we decided to label the casserole dish a science experiment rather than an example of total family laziness.

This and the dripping tap turning into the Avon Descent over a period of months really boil down to the same fact. We'd all like to think that if we ignore something for long enough, the situation will not only disappear of its own accord, but — most importantly — that no-one else will ever find out what mortifying secrets lie beneath the facade of a seemingly respectable and functional household.

The lambshank redemption

The only thing tastier than fast food is the smell of a slow dinner simmering in the family crockpot. In the morning, I pile sliced and diced vegetables, a kilo of lamb shanks, and some herbs and spices into a pan, turn it on low, go to work and in the evening come home to a house filled with the pungent aroma of perfect parenting.

It's self-righteous moments like these that offset the self-reproach felt when the family tucks into greasy cardboard boxes full of salt-laden chicken nuggets and chips — all while watching School-Canteen-Cop Jamie Oliver trying to enthuse a nation of unenthusiastic British children into discovering the health benefits of lunching on steamed cauliflower and broccoli. I've noticed that a good bottle of wine goes a looooong way to washing down any parental guilt I might be having difficulty swallowing while watching that gorgeous but sanctimonious git.

I want to be a positive role model like Jamie Oliver — bless his extensive organic herb garden, fruit trees, vegetable patch and army of paid workers — but my kids aren't interested in being positively role-modelled or eating anything lean and green or anything else of nutritional value. They just want sugar sandwiches after school.

Which also means the fresh selection of fruit sitting impressively in the large frosted glass bowl in the middle of our immaculate dining table ends up, after a couple of weeks, a rancid humming stew that smells like nail-polish remover — with a perfect halo of flies and insects circling above in an endless holding pattern.

This smells only slightly less offensive than my boys' end-of-term buzzing backpacks, which, upon parental examination, are revealed to have layer upon layer of scungy squashed salad sandwiches and black bananas eating away, like acid, the bottom of their school bags.

Unless, of course, my kids have binned their Mother-made sandwiches on the way to school, and whined, in a neglected and starving way, to the tired but trusting teacher on duty that they have no lunch — and could they please have a pie and sauce, and choc milk, from the canteen. I'm only privy to this little scheme when Welfare haul me out of work and hand me the canteen bill with a 'please explain' note attached.

Meanwhile, my boys are at home raiding the refrigerator, bypassing the fat- and sugar-free yoghurt selection, herbed cheese, carrot and celery sticks, in favour of stuffing themselves with crisps and white-bread tomato-sauce sandwiches.

My cooker's not the only thing that does a slow burn in our house.

Cake-mixed-up kids

I was happily lying in bed one morning when my husband came in and announced solemnly, 'The children are starving and we've run out of bread.' I thought about it for a moment, as waves of guilt crashed over me, and then, in a sudden blinding flash of inspiration, sat up and cried, 'Let them eat cakemix!'

Being a mother involves creativity, lateral thinking, a thick skin, nerves of steel and the ability to dissociate spontaneously at parent/teacher meetings. These allegedly hungry children are the same ones who, in less deprived times, think cookie dough and Fanta go together in the same way most adults believe barramundi goes better with a bottle of white wine. I was proud to realise that I'd discovered a lip-smacking alternative to boring old toast and shredded cardboard breakfast cereal

Raw cakemix, as we all know, tastes much better than actual cake, and highly refined white bread is exquisite when covered in lashings of real butter and sprinkled with sugar or hundreds and thousands. One morning, all that was left in the house was instant mashed potato and evaporated milk to start us on the way to work and school. It was a surprise hit with everyone and has appeared on our menu many times since.

Teenagers, and some adults, either by their nature, their hormones or simply because of anti-social rebelliousness, can have atrocious eating patterns, which then, like tax-return cheques, puppy fat and expensive school shoes, suddenly disappear or are grown out of fairly quickly. But my children apologise for letting down their side of the team when I've sometimes caught them eating apples, carrots and celery. Given the sheepish look they give me, I think they'd rather I'd caught them wearing my high-heeled shoes instead. It's very difficult for teenage insurgents to create family food wars when they're eating fruit and vegetables.

I can't be doing such a bad job, as my older son shot up ten centimetres overnight on a diet that mainly consisted of deep-fried onions, chewing gum, chicken nuggets, tomato sauce and plastic pen tops. Like the weeds in the cracks of our driveway, he's thriving on oily substances and harsh words.

The severest words are those I dish out when, during school holidays, I come home from a long, tiring day at work to find my two bum-crack boys watching *Quarantine*, and lying melded to our brand-new recliner rockers. Twin islands of brain death and belligerence in a sea of leftover fast food (including congealed and melted orange cheese), sticky lolly wrappers and crushed Coke cans, as well as tatty school bags, smelly shoes and even smellier socks, with an all-pervading fog of flatulence. I call it 'boysmell'.

In order to keep our sons suitably civilised, we occasionally take them out to dinner in Northbridge or to breakfast by the sea, for which they're forced not only to brush their teeth and hair but to brush up on their social skills as well. Here we can remind them of the subtle difference between using a knife and a fork and using grimy fingers. They can partake of Beef Wellington, rather than chomping on dried beef jerky in bed; Eggs Benedict instead of raw meringue mixture; and exquisitely decorated designer desserts as opposed to artificial dairy products from aerosol cans squirted fiercely, but lovingly, down each other's throats.

According to health experts, you should follow the 80/20 rule. Eat healthily 80 per cent of the time and the other 20 per cent, eat what you like. Whether my boys mainline their Maccas, snort refined white sugar or inhale cheese corn chips, they will, apparently, grow up healthily — well, 80 per cent of their bodies will. It's just the other 20 per cent I'm not sure about.

On yer bike

The Wild Child said to me, as she lay glued to the couch eating crisps in front of *The Simpsons*, that I was the laziest mother she had ever known.

So, I thought, I'll show her, and I signed up, with the SmartRider, for a 30-kilometre bike-hike marathon from Belmont to Joondalup.

The only exercise I'd had recently was walking from the TV to the fridge and back again several times a night — aside from,

I might add, a bit of elbow-bending down at the local. I spend as much time exercising as my daughter does cleaning out her bedroom.

I started off keenly enough, but by the time I hit the Polly Pipe, lactic acidosis had set in and I was feeling the Jane Fonda burn. And I was really jacked off when a guy in a converted wheelchair sailed effortlessly past me.

By the time I reached Osborne Park, I was the Last Man Standing, the Lone Ranger, Charlton Heston in *The Omega Man*, the only person left on Planet Earth. I Am NOT Legend, but my leg ends felt like they were falling off. There was even a straggly tumbleweed blowing silently across the freeway bitumen.

The wheelchair-bound guy had long since disappeared over the horizon and was probably enjoying a nice cup of tea on the far side of the finishing line. *The Simpsons* and a bag of crisps was starting to look very inviting indeed and I buoyed myself up by fantasising about roughly shoving my daughter off the couch.

My son had forged on ahead with ease. Thoroughly fed up with my stop/start, stop/start, I finally told him, in a scene reminiscent of the war movie *No-one Left Behind*, just to go on ahead without me. And he did. Ten minutes later, I got a text message, 'Are you OK, Mum?' I told him I was, as I lay on the side of the road gasping for an ambulance.

But I soldiered on limping slowly and made it as far as Erindale Road before I finally gave up, and waited for the big green bus that would pick up the fat and unfit, the lame and the infirm, and the ones with very sore body parts also suffering from a major injury to their dignity. I sat on half a bruised cheek in air-conditioned comfort for the last ten kilometres of the marathon.

By the time the bus got to the venue at the finishing line, all the entertainment was over and the band was packing up. Still, there's always next year. And if I can break the suction between my daughter and the couch, I'll be telling her, 'Next year, you're coming with me!'

Double dipping

Double dipping is not just about getting caught dunking your cheese cracker in the guacamole for the second time, it's also about children's ability to maximise their pocket money by scamming unsuspecting parents.

The ever so clever SmartRider double dips both his mother and father for his allowance on at least two separate occasions each week. Divide and conquer, and he's laughing all the way to the bank. But as we parents are bonded and united, by poverty, we have quickly wised up to our budding Gordon Gekko.

Greed is good — but not good enough. My kids are born con artists, grifters and swindlers and it's our job as custodians of their consciences to bash their developing brains with liberal servings of decency and honesty.

How else are they going to learn not to scam money for bus fares and lunches, then walk to school, go without nutritional sustenance at noon and pocket the difference? Despite our efforts, they seem to have more cash that they can possibly carry.

Some kids seem to spend a good part of their lives indulging in a wee bit of five-finger discounting at the local shops, goaded into action by peer pressure or, worse still, of their own volition.

When I was ten, I nicked some chocolate, and the shop owner gave me a very funny look on my way out. A week later she turned up on our doorstep and I nearly passed out.

Although I didn't know her, she knew my mum and her visit wasn't about me at all. I still suffer post-traumatic stress disorder due to my guilty conscience, though. These days, if your kids get caught pilfering from the aisles, it's not just internal shame that can punish them over a lifetime — their security tape could end up on *The World's Stupidest Shoplifters*.

Most adults have at some stage justified to themselves their fetish for office stationery when they've caused a few pens to go missing. It's only when you come home with a computer or a photocopier tucked under your jumper, or a fax machine hidden in your handbag, that a twelve-step group might be an idea.

A child's sense of entitlement also seems to stretch to the loose change down the sides of couches, at the bottoms of washing machines and on their father's bedside table. One of my children, who shall remain nameless, amasses this treasure trove, asks me what I want from the shops — bread, milk or Valium — pays for it with illicit bounty, gets a receipt and demands reimbursement. Correct me if I am wrong, but, in the language of *The Sopranos*, isn't that called 'laundering'? At least he's washing something, I sigh.

Rather like the time I found 20 dollars, at a time when this represented half my weekly pay packet, on the carpet of a well-known banking institution and, with racing pulse and high anxiety, snatched and ran faster than an ATM can swallow a stolen credit card.

Money talks. In fact, it screams loudly in our house. This is especially so down the end where the SmartRider lives. It might not come as a surprise to learn he wants to become an accountant. Now, what's Tony Soprano's number again?

Extreme eating

My younger son is currently going through the dreaded vegetarian phase. Only, it's a phase that's lasting longer than we thought it would. Except to bite my head off on various occasions, meat hasn't passed his lips for the best part of three years. Yes, three years.

Now, that's not bad considering we haven't made any concessions for him. He simply gets served up the vegetable portion of whatever I cook and baked beans gets added to his meal. We also make a huge deal of letting him know just how delicious the dead animals on our plate are. What we'd really like is for his eating habits simply to conform in to the rest of the family's and make my life a lot easier.

As a rabid carnivore, I find eating only vegetable matter akin to having foreplay without the sex. Unless there's meat on the plate, it doesn't feel like a satisfying meal.

But he's a very happy chappy and seems to thrive on a diet devoid of animals. He hasn't lost vast amounts of weight, as I erroneously predicted, and his energy levels are still the same, as can be seen in his ability to wind me up on a regular basis.

I can't see his vegetarianism coming to an end soon either. He's always been a stubborn, obsessive-compulsive little blighter and is the only child of mine who always hangs up wet towels on the bathroom rack and washes his hands after he goes to the toilet — even at three o'clock in the morning.

My daughter went through her vegetarian phase a few years ago and it lasted until we got Red Rooster for dinner that night. Her motives were less pure than my son's, though, as she embarked on it to win a bet with her friends. She lost. My son is doing it because he genuinely believes in not eating anything that was previously alive (rather like the limp carrots I serve him).

There is as much chance that I, on the other hand, will give up meat as there is that I will turn to wrestling grizzly bears for a living or tackle the pile of extreme ironing that's taken up residence in the laundry. For me, a meal without meat is like a pub with no beer.

But, as much as I'm frustrated, and slightly guilt ridden at feeling that I don't provide adequate sustenance for my growing youngest son, I have to admire him for his beliefs and discipline. Reluctantly and almost begrudgingly, I've dug out a vegetarian stir-fry book and plan on having a few meat-free meals, but I think first of all a trip to KFC is well in order. We can eat the chicken and he can have the eleven herbs and spices. It's called a win/win situation.

Cashed-up kids sending us broke

Just when we think we can make ends meet, someone moves the goal posts. I woke up one morning to discover three huge, ravenous teenage children had suddenly invaded my house. That's when the goal posts suddenly ripped apart harder and faster than a turkey slap on a reality TV show.

However, if you were lucky enough to give birth recently you would have passed Go and collected the baby bonus from the

Australian Government, just for producing another little Aussie sprog. But just how far will this take you? The cost of nappies used to send me completely potty, and I found the best formula for saving money was to breast-feed.

It was far more cost-effective to invest in a couple of Wiggles videos than put the kids into child care. I discovered that while pots and pans and metal spoons as toys might cost nothing, I would have to invest in a couple of ear plugs, which saved my sanity as I spent several years listening to three successive toddlers happily banging away for hours on end.

The cost of five veg and three fruit — times five people — times seven days a week, is enough to make me want to live on Soylent Green for the rest of my life. For a week's shop we don't get past the checkout for under the cost of a modest four-door sedan. Add to that the twin necessities of family life, that is, headache tablets and two-litre casks of wine, and we've blown out the budget so high that it's shot past the stratosphere and split the universe.

Another way to haemorrhage 100-dollar notes is to take a trip to the cinema to watch a bad movie. For us, though, that's still cheaper than hiring a good DVD because we are so feckless about returning them on time. There are several video shops in our area with bounties on our heads for unpaid fines.

For his birthday we bought the SmartRider an expensive Nintendo DS with a game called 'Labradogs', through which he gets to care and bond with an electronic pet while actively ignoring the real one sitting hungry and neglected with her face pressed up against the glass of the back door.

Designer t-shirts hang off the children's backs and name-brand sneakers dirty up my couch as they lie in front of the TV, plugged into their iPods, or MP3s, whatever they are. You either have kids or money or a clean couch, but never all three at the same time.

Next time you find yourself destitute, don't hock your grandmother's wedding ring at Cash Converters. Instead, grab a bottle of wine and some massage oil, and have an early night. And nine months later, you'll be laughing, crying or writhing in agony — all the way to the bank.

You are what your mother ate

Just when you thought it was safe to come out of the kitchen, along comes yet ANOTHER government-funded mother-maligning medical report, loading you with enough guilt to send you scurrying back to the pantry for some maternal comfort in the shape of an illicit supply of Mars Bars and cream buns.

According to 'new Australian research', you are what your mother and grandmother ate. Apparently, lifestyle choices, such as your diet during pregnancy, directly affects the future health of at least the next two generations.

In another recent report I read that, while the father influences the child's height, the mother determines their fatness. This could explain why we have three short, plump children in our household.

During my pregnancies, I craved all acidic, piquant foodstuffs such as capsicum, olives and lemons, which, rather like my children, are considered to be an acquired taste. This could also explain why my offspring are a bunch of sourpusses when asked to do anything that doesn't involve eating, drinking or watching TV.

As well, I used to eat brick dust while I was pregnant. My husband often used to find me in the middle of the night grinding up our feature brick wall with my teeth. More than a decade down the track, when their teachers ring me up to say that my kids are as thick as two bricks, I tend to take it personally.

But, while it's rather difficult to get a broad backside from a bunch of beige-coloured bricks, it would appear there *are* kilojoules in genes, because, according to the aforementioned research, genes cause obesity. You won't get an argument from me there. Ever tried to squeeze a size sixteen body into a pair of size twelve jeans in a changing cubicle no bigger than a box of Froot Loops?

Once again, thanks to the rich plethora of parent-bashing boffins, I can freely blame my father for my shortcomings and my mother for my fat comings. In turn, my children can lie on the couch with their noses in a bag of Burger Rings and tell me it's not *their* fault, it's *my* fault. And I can lie back with a clear conscience and argue that it's not *my* fault either. The blame, as usual, lies fairly and squarely with *my* parents.

My friend, the chocolate cake

I was always in a hurry for my kids to grow up so that I could be friends with them. They were cute as babies and toddlers, but I knew the real communication would start when they were older, and got opinions, attitude and part-time jobs. I nursed the warm inner conviction that dinnertime conversation would centre on well-thought-out answers to the question of the meaning of life and philosophical discussions about why books are always better than television.

So, it was a rude awakening to discover that my kids were far more interested in watching the semi-naked shenanigans of *Big Brother* through the reflection of the games room window while posh noshing on sausages and mash at the dinner table, than they were in discussing how the universe was created. Or why George Orwell would shudder at the thought of a group of horny young adults locked together while an allegedly cultured country watches every move they make.

This is, unless their friends are staying for dinner. Then, lingering at the dinner table is seen as wicked fun, particularly if I produce a chocolate cake or a packet of Tim Tams. Not that I'm trying to lull them into a false sense of security where they feel safe to confess any shortcomings or anything, but it's been my experience that chocolate has far more truth-extraction power than does an injection of truth serum.

If you want to find out what's happening in Teenage-Land, keep your own mouth occupied with rich, blood-pressure reducing, antioxidant-rich dark chocolate, and just communicate your parental wisdom through a series of non-threatening nods and grunts. It's always good to suppress anxiety levels with fat kilojoules when they tell you stuff that's usually relegated to the front-page headlines of tabloid newspapers.

Some kids give their parents a wide berth on extra-parental activities, but mine feel the need to go into minute detail that's way too much information for my hardened arteries and dicky heart. But forewarned is forearmed and knowledge is power.

Then there are the kids who tell their parents absolutely nothing. It was only when we had a knock on the door at four o'clock one Sunday morning and opened it to see a pair of burly policemen on our doorstep, that we realised one of our teenage house guests had somehow forgotten to tell his parents he wouldn't be home that night. This was a scary situation that no amount of chocolate cake was ever going to sort out.

Culture shock

The difference between an exclusive restaurant and the place where my daughter is earning her apprentice chef stripes can be judged not only by the outrageously inflated prices at the first of these, but by the amount — or lack thereof — of chilled chardonnay poured into a wine glass.

Posh restaurant waiters twirl the white-napkined wine bottle and fill the glass to just under a third, before retreating with a bow and extravagant rolling hand gestures. Where my daughter works, cheap house wine is generously sloshed into a balloon glass until a skin bubble appears over the rim.

It's a mother's duty to introduce her Emo Grunge daughter into the finer things of life whether she wants a cultural education or not. So, I took mine out, leaving our three males behind, for a fine dining and female bonding experience. We went up 33 floors to a revolving restaurant that affords a magnificent 360-degree view of the night lights of Perth.

But before that we had to address the issue of what to wear. Or, more precisely, what not to wear. Strict dress standards applied and I was worried my Kmart togs weren't quite up to scratch.

However, it's even harder to find something suitable, and clean, to wear when, as in the case of my daughter, everything you own is strewn over your cluttered bedroom floor like seaweed over a windswept Coogee Beach. So, I suggested she check out my wardrobe instead. Seeing as everything I own is either pink and glittery, pink and flowery, or pink, glittery and flowery, the idea of Daughter wearing my clothes is a bit like Elvira, Mistress of Darkness, borrowing an outfit from Olivia Newton-John.

But while she might have been unexcited by my wardrobe, she was, being a chef, blown away by the pristine kitchen facilities, and spent more time drooling over the oven than she did over the gorgeous Andrew-G-lookalike waiter who served us.

This was not the sort of place you could request a doggie bag, even if your main course of lobster cost more than the lounge suite the rest of the family, back in the Northern Suburbs, were eating their Red Rooster off. So, although I was tempted to slide the leftover crustacean discreetly into my handbag, embarrassing my daughter was not on the menu. The meal might have cost an arm, a leg and a couple of kidneys, but finally impressing my unimpressible teenage daughter was absolutely priceless.

3

Q. Should children clean their bedroom before saving the planet?

A. EVEN AL GORE HID CRUSTY UNDERWEAR AND MILK-FILLED CEREAL BOWLS UNDER THE BED.

An inconvenient truth about boys

If Al Gore, in his spare time, can scour the world into global cooling, you'd think it wouldn't be too difficult for me to swab the decks of my younger son's bedroom.

So, I marched in armed with elbow-length gloves, breathing mask, industrial-strength bleach, ceiling scraper and single-minded doggedness, because trying to get this son to tidy up his bedroom is like trying to get a pooch to bury its own droppings.

An inconvenient truth about teenage boys is that they are mucky, smelly cave-dwelling Missing Linkers who attract more dirt than the entire Britney Spears clan put together. I'll bet that even Al Gore used to throw dried beef jerky sticks and stiff crusty socks and jocks under his bed before he grew up and decided to save the world single-handedly after Superman died.

While what was under my son's bed might've been lifting it a metre off the carpet, at least there weren't tall columns of yellowing newspapers hiding a *Today Tonight* camera crew intent on sniffing out yet another neglectful mother of a suburban obsessive-compulsive control freak. Empty cereal packets and plastic milk containers were also hidden in the wardrobe and there was enough to fill the hole in the ozone layer.

Said hole is about the same size as the hole I was drilling into my son's head with a red-hot poker. I wasn't so much cleaning his room as lifting the lid off his skull, delving into the deep, dark corners, and scooping out the remains of his self-esteem and childhood memories. He just wanted me out of his bedroom, his head and his life, and cried that I should just kill him quickly and get it over and done with, instead of this slow torture.

Every single slater-chewed bus ticket, M&M wrapper, Patsy Biscoe tape, Nikki Webster CD, desiccated spider dropping and ebola-carrying cock-roaches had to be delicately and meticulously negotiated over. When I pulled out from behind his book case several pairs of dirty underwear (why is it always DIRTY underwear?) held together with duct tape, I lost the will to live, sat down, repeatedly banged my head against the wall and had a good cry (something you don't see Al Gore doing very often, or, at least, not in public).

Crying might not solve global warming, but my frozen heart thawed considerably when my son made me a cup of tea and told me that he loved his newly clean room. What is it about your children that makes you want to slap them with one hand and cuddle them with the other?

The Darwin awards

Teenage boys are proof positive that the evolutionary process can sometimes work in reverse.

A good example of 'Survival of the Thickest' in our household is the Dreamer trying to gain my attention by continuously flicking my right ear with his finger as I'm sitting down at the breakfast table, enjoying my first cup of percolated coffee before heading off for work.

A Darwinian act is anything that is not conducive to the survival of the species. Even the cat's a Darwinian contender when, in the middle of the night, she scratches at our bedroom door to go out when ten minutes earlier she had wanted to come in. If she were a smart cat, she'd learn either to reach up and turn the brass handle herself or morph silently through the varnished wood into the hallway.

If my boys were less reverse-evolutionally-challenged, they would learn NOT to pick fights with each other just as I get home from work and NEVER, EVER to leave the cold-water jug sitting out on the kitchen bench so that I'm forced to drink warm tap water on a 45 degree day. Other fatal instincts my teenage boys display are the ones to change the channel while *Desperate Housewives* is on, talk over the news, raid the fridge five minutes before dinner and call out 'Are you awake?!' when clearly I am fast asleep on the couch.

Charles Darwin, on the other hand, would be proud of my husband's ability to adapt favourably to pressurised circumstances. During my third pregnancy, my husband decided to get his pilot's licence, which meant flying around the skies above Jandakot Airport every Saturday and Sunday while I looked after two active toddlers.

One evening when I was nine-and-a-half months pregnant with number three, he came home, surveyed the scene, and commented that the place was 'a bit of a pigsty.' He has since learned that the correct evolutionary response to a dirty house is: 'Here's a bunch of very expensive flowers, dear! I'll now make you a cup of tea, massage your sore back with one hand and do the dishes with the other!'

However, the ultimate winner of our own Darwin Awards is the person who stole the last rocky road Drumstick from the freezer when I'd been hanging out for a chocolate fix all day. He was smart enough to snaffle the goods undetected, but dumb enough to leave the wrapper lying on his bedside table.

Domestos goddess

My younger son the SmartRider is on a mission — to clean up our suburb. He might find cleaning his teeth or his bedroom floor Mission: Impossible, but after school he regularly does his own personal tour of scab duty around the streets. He also revels in his new role of unmitigated martyrdom.

What is it with kids who desperately want to save the world but can't be bothered saving their parents an expensive dental bill by regularly cleaning the yellow gunge off their teeth?

When our son comes home full of pride, with his head wider and larger than the bagful of street rubbish he's dragging behind him, I mention that perhaps he could be just as personally fulfilled by introducing his teeth to Mr Toothbrush. He looks at me as if I'm a mutant from *Planet Talking Out of Uranus*.

So does my other son, who, when asked to clean up his room on Psycho Saturday, simply parts the Red Sea of the debris on his carpet, claims he's finished, and gets all aggressive and moody when I point out I've seen less rubbish on free-to-air TV on a Saturday night.

My daughter would happily wash up dishes at a local restaurant but baulks at the idea of wiping down a bench in her own home. But all this is normal behaviour, I am told by my parents who tell me that I was exactly the same.

For the purposes of parenting, I have reinvented myself as the perfect teenager who didn't leave cereal bowls and apple cores under the bed, who did the dishes the first time she was asked, and made her parents breakfast in bed every Sunday morning before scrubbing the scullery, polishing the silver and blacking the fireplace. My kids look at me skeptically when I thus regale them. So does my mother.

Skeptical was also the way I looked at the Wild Child on the one and only occasion she cleaned the bathroom, then got homicidal when her brothers spat toothpaste on the mirror and left wet towels on the floor. She complained bitterly about their apathy, but my care factor was lower than the black mould on the shower floor that she had failed to notice.

Years ago, when the only mould in my house was on the blue-veined cheese, I was considered a Domestos Goddess. My first post-having-children job, was a cleaning one and my children said, with wide, glowing eyes, that I must really love cleaning if I were willing to be gainfully employed as a cleaner.

I used to think I was the Queen of Clean — then it finally dawned on me that I was just another worn-out old scrubber.

Shadow dancing

Scratch the surface of any seemingly mature, well-adjusted human being and underneath lurks the potential for a raging psychopathic monster.

Such was the case one morning when I was driving to work in a peaceful Buddhist meditative mood, and decided to pull out from the left-hand lane into the right-hand one, indicating at the same time I turned the steering wheel. As one does. The driver of the car behind me in the right-hand lane slammed on the brakes, and the man in my rear-view mirror threw up his hands in a gesture of annoyance and frustration. My instinctive, primordial reaction was to jerk my well-manicured middle finger up and down violently, screaming a string of expletives that would make Belinda Neal blush furiously.

But it was not me gesticulating uncontrollably — it was my shadow. We all have one. A dark side to our personalities, in which vengeful monsters lurk in wait for the optimally stressful moment to emerge, howling and baying ferociously into the wind.

Just ask Mel Gibson, or even Jack Nicholson, who once swiped at someone's limousine with a golf club, later stating in court that he had mistaken it for a golf ball. Or you could ask the mother who bailed up the Dreamer's teacher in the school car park and threatened him with bodily harm because her son was, quite rightly, sent home early from school camp for very bad behaviour.

There's nothing quite like observing a public dummy-spit to bring out the *schadenfraude* in all of us. Schadenfreude is when ordinary, everyday citizens revel in the other people's misfortunes and their consequent misery and sorrow. (Which reminds me — there's a family gathering looming on the horizon.)

Schadenfraude accurately describes the through-a-glass-darkly side of a quiet and passive overweight person who gets a kick out of seeing someone else gain a considerable amount of kilos while purportedly living on a diet of grapefruit and rice crackers for several months. It also describes the feeling upon seeing an arrogant P-plated maniac fuming on the side of the road while copping a speeding fine from a couple of burly policemen just shortly after he'd overtaken you in a cloud of smoke for going too slow.

Thank goodness these policemen were not around at eight o'clock on a recent Monday morning. Note to the nice-looking man in a white shirt in my rear-view mirror who was driving a blue car down the Reid Highway, minding his own business when I cut him off — it really wasn't your fault! But you knew that all along! Didn't you?

Faring well without welfare

Britney Spears and I have a lot in common. Aside from blonde hair and a tendency to a well-deserved spare-tyre, we both have an overwhelming fear of Welfare banging down our front door in the middle of the night. Here are some very good reasons I'm worried they have us pencilled in for a visit in the very near future.

First up, there's Cracked Pepper. Apparently, it is not merely a condiment, it's a flammable substance suitable for creating a very impressive fireworks display in your kitchen. All you have to do is toss a handful of the stuff at your gas hotplates and, *voila* — you have your own indoors Perth Sky Show. (Too much fun can also be had turning a deodorant can into a flame-thrower, with the aid of some enthusiastic hands and a match. Not even chasing my delinquent children around the house with a wooden spoon was an adequate deterrent.)

Then there's Incriminating Photos. It only takes a camera, a black marker pen, a cigarette and three feral children for you to discover that you don't have extremely naughty children on your hands. Instead, you have creative geniuses, who, demonstrating great artistic talent, have drawn a cheeky face on the youngest child's bum, and stuck a cigarette between the cheeks for extra effect. (I'm just grateful they didn't light it first, especially as he lived on baked beans at the time.) The roll of film was submitted to and processed by the chemist, but somehow the mooning shots they assured me they'd taken weren't returned. I decided not to pursue the matter. Neither did the police.

Then there's the Number One reason we fear Welfare will give us a wake-up call. Our teenage daughter promised us, and we believed her, that she would NOT, under any circumstances throw the traditional 'My-Parents-Are-Out-of-Town Party' when we left her Home Alone for the weekend while the rest of us camped down south.

The smoking gun was NOT our coffee cups being used as ashtrays, or the beer and vodka cruiser bottles left lying around the back garden, or even the teenager-shaped hole in our fly-screen door, which someone had broken through in order to heave up a Pro Hart imitation on our brick paving. No! It was the party animal who text messaged my mobile phone instead of my daughter's, with 'GR8 party, on again tonight?'

By the time we got back, our daughter had done a bunk and was staying the night at a friend's house. If I'd got hold of her then, Welfare would not just have been banging on our door, they would have been chasing me down the street with a wooden spoon.

The joys of bombs, bills and boys

Each day when I wearily get home from work, I check the letterbox, only to find it full of bills and threatening final-demand letters.

I used to get lovely long letters from overseas relatives and now all I get are seemingly innocuous window-faced envelopes, which turn out to contain warnings written in blood and bold type that if we don't pay so-and-so within seven days, they'll send someone round to legally break my favourite teddy bear's legs.

Last week, someone blew up our letterbox. Unfortunately, they disappeared before I had a chance to thank them. The result was a round letterbox where a square one had existed previously. It reminded me a bit of the guy in the mouthwash advert who swigs down a capful of Semtex and blows his cheeks apart.

More to the point was that both my boys somehow knew exactly the technical specifications of blowing up letterboxes. Apparently, it involved a pile of gunpowder shavings and a standing sparkler, which gave off enough blast power to blow the lid off our letterbox and launch it into orbit, where it replaced poor, maligned Pluto as the ninth planet circling the sun.

But seemingly it takes more than Osama bin Laden to stop Australia Post delivering the mail. As well as continuing to receive council, land and water rates, we now have to finance my first-born son taking a trip to England, where he and 39 other acoustically inclined students will perform concerts for lots of lucky Londoners.

In order to help with costs, he applied for a newspaper round. Inevitably, my younger son then wanted one too, but was legally not of age. So, we decided that caring and sharing the paper round was the way to go.

Two headstrong boys into one newspaper round should equate to half of one each but, for a while there, all it added up to was frazzled nerves, loud voices, and plenty of personal insults. Seeing as in our household dividing chocolate involves a sharp knife and a pair of kitchen scales, I had to have the wisdom of King Solomon to produce two content and cooperative members of the male species from one entrepreneurial venture. They got to appreciate many letterboxes, including the remains of own, while doing their round and managed not to blow each other up in the process.

And to the person who exploded ours: next time, make sure you do the job properly.

Sheds and garages

There are things around a house only a woman can do properly and there are things around the garage and shed that only a man can stuff up, and never the twain shall meet. This is why when the garage needed cleaning out, I told my husband it was in his job description as a bloke and not in mine as a woman.

His reply: 'You don't need a dick to clean out the garage.' Be that as it may, darling, one does not need to wear a bra to scrub out the toilet either.

My two boys might run a mile when there are dishes to be done but fight over who's going to mow the lawn this week, while my daughter and I are more interested in defoliating our legs and armpits than we are in deforesting the back garden. We don't suffer from lawnmower envy.

So, while Daughter and I went shopping, lunching and to the movies, my man about the house proceeded to clean up the garage. This really meant moving all the junk from one side to the other. In other words, he gave it a 'bloke's clean' which is the same principle as a 'bloke's look' in the fridge when he can't find the milk while making me a cup of tea. It's funny, but I've never heard my husband say, 'Honey, I can't find my beer in the fridge.'

This is rather like the way my two boys can locate with x-ray vision a certain screwdriver amongst thousands in a dark, dingy shed, but on a Monday morning cannot find their school clothes, which I've cleverly concealed on top of the bed.

Once, while on a child-and-husband-free holiday in Brisbane, I received a call on my mobile phone from my husband asking me the whereabouts of our elder son's scout uniform. It would appear that self-sufficiency is sometimes in insufficient quantities in our house, regardless of what blokey bits one has or hasn't got. So, I felt great trepidation recently when a co-worker's car broke down, in the rain, after hours, with no man to be found, and I was the bunny with the jumper leads in the boot.

But within ten minutes her car was off and running, leaving me with the thought that, while I might not possess a male appendage, I managed to do a pretty good man's job.

If you can't do the time

The other day my daughter was deliberately annoying her younger brother and shredding my nerves in the process. As punishment, I told her to get to her room. She looked at me, laughed and said, 'I'm eighteen, I don't go to my room.' So I locked myself in my bedroom instead for a well-deserved timeout standing in the corner facing the wall.

Just how do you punish your adult children? I can't stop her pocket money: she now works full-time and earns more than I do. I can't ground her: she just thumbs her nose and walks out the door faster than you can say 'Super Nanny'.

Back in the good old days, I would chase my naughty children round the dining-room table with a wooden spoon. On one occasion I hunted them down and whacked them with the sharp side of the Glad Wrap box (something, I'm sure, they'll be telling their therapist, or parole officer, in the years to come).

My inconsistent mothering skills make Joan Crawford look like Carol Brady. These days, I seem to yell more empty threats than a politician shouts empty promises at election time. And they know it.

Still, one effective technique if my kids misbehave in the car, is to lock the radio onto AM talkback. They end up bored rigid, which leads to compliant apathy every time. It's a win–lose situation that works for me, unlike what happened at the supermarket.

One day an old codger, who had obviously never taken three children under five for a weekly food shop, gave me a lot of grief when I lost it and threatened to abandon my kids. With one toddler hugging my kneecap in the manner of a boa constrictor, the four year old throwing up in aisle five and the baby screaming for a breast-feed, I told him as politely as I could, given the circumstances, exactly where he could stick his unwanted advice. He disappeared quicker than a bag of lollies at a birthday party, muttering something under his breath about bad mothers and future psychopaths.

So far, I haven't produced any serial killers or school shooters. But it's difficult to punish a child these days without them screaming about their human rights and threatening to call the United Nations. The school system, FM radio, *Big Brother* and growth hormones in chickens have a lot to answer for.

My rebuttal to them is that kids need discipline like a parent needs a drink and lots of personal space after a long day at the office. As I tell my little cherubs, the Geneva Convention works both ways, darlings!

She drives me crazy

I bought a new car in the same week my Wild Child got her learner's permit. She now thinks that MY new car is jointly owned.

After the future Princess P-Plater greeted me with the news that sends icy waves of fear into every parent's heart, she wanted to take me and my nerves, for a test spin around the block. I grabbed some Prozac, a bottle of vodka and a crash helmet, and she grabbed her favourite grunge band's CD, apparently under the impression that ear-splitting music was conducive to successful three-point turns and parallel parking. It was more likely, of course, that she wanted to be able to drown out my shrill, nagging voice just as I wanted to drown out my overwhelming fear with mind-altering substances.

This was not my daughter's first driving experience. The same long weekend that we went camping and she threw an unauthorised party, we had left her in charge of the house, the cats, the dog, the goldfish and the aging family station wagon. Whereupon my licensed trustworthy car, driven by my unlicensed, untrustworthy daughter and her scaly mates, was used for a Saturday-night-pizza purchasing pursuit 23 suburbs away.

Sometime in the last century when I got my learner's permit, I drove my mother to drink by kangaroo-hopping her manual car all the way down Mundaring Weir Road one day. I still have ongoing medical issues from Mum screaming into my left eardrum every time a car passed in the opposite direction and the road was very busy that day.

And the first night I drove alone to the local roller-skating rink, it was in a very busy and extremely full car park that, upon leaving, I managed to reverse into another car and shatter its headlight, and then, in the grip of a major panic attack, took off like a bat out of hell. It cost me two weeks' wages to get the back of Mum's car repaired.

Upon telling my daughter this story, she replied that something like that would never happen to her. She then reversed out of the driveway in my brand-new baby-blue Barina faster than Lindsay Lohan entering and exiting rehab, the g-forces stretching the wrinkles to the sides of my bloodless face and making me look, but not feel, 30 years younger.

As with my mother and I, and countless others before us, this was our first and last attempt at mother–daughter bonding through driving experiences. Such stories are also the reason there are several thousand entries in the *Yellow Pages* for very expensive driving schools.

Saving the whales

Saving the Whales isn't about rescuing randy royals from the intrusiveness of the English tabloids. It's all about the awakening of a social conscience in my impressionable teenage daughter, who recently attended her first environmental awareness meeting, thanks to a glossy pamphlet handed out by a random street person. With the promise of rapturous rallies and police-provoking parades, it ignited in her a passionate fire even the most evangelistic zealot would envy.

The first environmentally friendly person who greeted my hygiene-conscious Wild Child was wearing a tank top, and sporting a bird's nest, of albatross proportions, under each arm. The owner of these Afro-armpits was propped up by a pair of unashamedly unshaven legs. While offending my daughter's senses, all this did not override her devotion to the cause but was still something she and her attending friend just weren't going to get over in a hurry. Had I not let her go to the meeting, my daughter would still be banging on about dobbing me into Welfare for violating her human rights, so, for the sake of a peaceful life, I let her find out for herself what I already knew — that people who want to save the rainforests never defoliate anything, anywhere, anytime.

I, of course, also have a vegetarian son with Buddhist leanings, who wouldn't dream of stepping on an ant or swatting a fly but feels not an ounce of anguish every time he kicks his brother in the shins. This is the same son who bends my ears about the ethics of stem cell research at the dinner table while eating his meat-free meal, and who manages to imbue me with extreme guilt every time I buy fast-food chicken and chips.

And, again regarding the environment, while I stopped throwing cigarette butts and chocolate wrappers out the car window a long time ago, I still haven't got into the habit of recycling anything — unless turning old chardonnay bottles into waxy multi-coloured candle-holders counts for something. This is about to change, with the advent of our local shire kindly donating our first recycling bin. Just what I need — more grunt work in the kitchen. But I came to the conclusion that, while my bench top might be dirty, at least my soul will be scrubbed immaculately clean.

Saving the planet is something we should all think about, and, as a mother and a life-long member of Planet Earth I intend to do so, but, at the same time, I think I need to save my children from themselves. Or is it the other way round?

4

Q. Why is it easier to Facebook than to get your teen's face in a book?

A. IT'S HARD WORK EDUCATING THE INDIFFERENT TO MAKE A DIFFERENCE.

For whom the school bell tolls

The key to success is education. But if school years are wasted on the little people at the pointy end of their lives, it's eagerly embraced and ferociously devoured by the over-40s facing the blunt end of existence. Because, according to the latest neuroscience research, it's possible for your brain to give birth to new cells. So, apparently, you CAN flog a dead horse and bring it back to life.

Neuroplasticity is the name for the ability to regenerate neurons through new experiences, a process that can be accelerated through repetitive learning even by someone who is effectively brain-dead. That is, someone who gave birth to three children and rejoined the work force after ten years of scrubbing floors and cleaning toilets.

The death and rebirth of brain matter is rather like sticking your chewing gum on the bedpost overnight. In the still night air it sets like concrete in its dark, dank confines. But in the morning, with some dedicated rumination, not only is its flavour still evident but the gum can be shaped and stretched in any direction you might want it to go. Dead grey matter can also be reconstituted with a little bit of effort, such as doing crosswords or Sudoko, or even reading the latest Harry Potter book. Neuroplasticity is not so much brainwashing as it is brain spit and polishing.

All this just goes to show that you CAN teach an old dog new tricks, but the challenge in education these days is how to teach a new dog new tricks.

If I crank up the time machine and go back to 1979, my Tertiary Entrance Exam year, my perception of the irrelevance of my education is highlighted by my memory of my long-suffering history teacher trying to educate this recalcitrant student about French foreign policy between the two World Wars. I felt that it had about as much bearing on my then everyday life as Hillary Clinton's alleged cleavage has had on American politics today.

Beating the education drum loudly and clearly to today's youth doesn't mean they necessarily hear the important message being sent any more than I did. After stumbling around for a couple of years in post-TEE wilderness before finally getting accepted into university, my friend's son lamented to her, in a highly critical tone, 'Why didn't you tell me about the value of education?'

Suspending reality

One day at work I got a phone call from the deputy principal of my elder son's high school informing me that he had been suspended for two days. When I got home that night I said to the boy, without a hint of anger or sarcasm, 'Congratulations! Your father and I are very proud of you.'

And we were. After continually being bullied in Year Seven, he finally stood up for himself, fighting back when another boy punched him. And, as I told the deputy principal in no uncertain terms, my son should have been awarded a medal for bravery.

According to school policy, however, he should have turned tail, run to the staffroom and dobbed in the other boy because, the education department says, 'conflict resolution should always occur in a non-violent, safely contained, teacher-controlled environment'. The last time we tried cosy fireside counselling chats with unrepentant bullies, they, surprisingly enough, didn't work. Afterwards, we secretly told our son to snot the bully on the nose but 'only if he hits you first'.

It's been my experience, and the experience of other mothers, that most testosterone-charged teenage boys resolve conflict with their fists and feet in an unsafe, non-contained and teacher-free environment. It's the only language that teenage boys understand when the testosterone rises up in them like a tsunami.

This doesn't mean that any male who's ever thrown a punch is going to end up with a broken nose, cauliflower ears and a Mike Tyson mentality. Even my gentle, peace-loving husband used to give his younger brother a bloody nose and a well-warranted thump on a regular basis.

Boys throw a few punches, shed some blood, shake hands, drink beer, call each other 'mate' a lot and get over it. Girls fight too. But, instead of a bloody nose, they give each other eating disorders, self-harm tendencies, panic attacks, low self-esteem coupled with high anxiety and suicide-ideation, start a cold war that divides the classroom and are still sobbing in their therapist's office 20 years down the track. Boys proudly bear their scars as badges of honour, while girls tend to bleed to death internally.

And somehow we mothers have to take this burden of our warring children on our shoulders as well as working full-time. So, while I wanted to go and see this other boy who threw the first punch and sort out his mother, there really wasn't any point, because the next week not only were he and my son good friends again but he was round at our house, playing pool, drinking Coke and raiding our fridge. Fight! What fight?!

Homework, Homer Simpson style

Homework is like cleaning the oven, I say to my children: it's a job that has to be done whether you like it or not. I also tell them that there are certain therapeutic benefits to doing a job well (either that, or the oven-cleaning chemicals I use are making me high).

Of course, that sort of parent-speak is lost on a child who has homework to complete on a sunny Saturday afternoon when playing football, riding bikes and burning down the local bushland beckon.

If the children have three hours' homework, I set aside four for the duration. This is to take account of the first hour being spent moaning, groaning, and thrashing around complaining of an allegedly sore writing hand or imaginary headache in a bid to convince me to write a note to the teacher explaining why the dog ate their homework.

Back in my day, there was more chance of me marrying one of the Bay City Rollers than there was of parental involvement with my homework assignments, not that I did very many of those.

Most of my angst-ridden adolescence was spent languishing on my bed, mooning over giant-sized posters of Eric, Les and Woody, and writing long, detailed stories about what I'd like to do with them should they ever suddenly materialise in my life.

My daughter, who has no interest in marrying one of the Bay City Rollers, when she was at school preferred arguing me into a rabid frothing-mouthed frenzy, resulting in a loss of pocket money and privileges, rather than just knuckling down and getting on with homework.

I could sympathise with her, though, not that I ever let on. Given the choice when sorting out in a desperate manner the family's finances, I would rather sit down with a large bag of Maltesers and a good book.

The Dreamer, who used to want to marry Nikki Webster, recently had a major homework assignment on the Commonwealth Games. After several weeks of procrastination, it was resolved in a time-honoured manner acceptable to both parties. That is, we had the mother of all arguments, in which we brought up major issues from the past and accused each other of being a moron, and I told him to go and watch TV and I'd do the entire assignment for him. And he did and I did. And we all lived happily ever after.

Well, until the next homework assignment came along, that is.

The wheels on the bus go round and round

There is nothing on earth that induces in me more unmitigated terror than spotting a bus full of those sadistic creatures known as high school students. It may be a bright, sunny day but dark clouds suddenly rain down acid 1970s memories in which getting tortured by Idi Amin was preferable to catching the school bus home.

Whoever said schooldays are the best days of one's life has either had a frontal lobotomy or years of regressive psychotherapy, or was home-schooled by a clingy mother. Or all three. When I was at school, if you had red hair and freckles, were a nerd, a fatty or a four-eyes, you always attracted unwanted attention from the kids who preyed upon those lower down the food chain than them.

My daughter was explaining, in graphic detail, to the SmartRider about that mobile torture chamber known as the school bus, and it would appear that the unwritten rules haven't changed over the decades. The really scary kids, ie, the ones who will potentially shoot up the school, the other psychopaths, the druggies and the cool dudes, sit on the back seats; the gorgeous but plastic Barbie dolls sit in front of them; and the normal kids sit in the middle. The weakest links either stand in the aisle or hang around the front somewhere in the Bermuda Triangle of the bus driver, the yellow line and the automatic door. The bullies are at the back and the bullied are at the front. When everyone knows their place, harmony reigns and it's a smooth ride. However, the ramifications are severe if you end up sitting in the wrong seat. Eggs, half-eaten apples and 'water' balloons containing fluid other than water, get hurled at the back of your head, and your backpack (formerly the old grey school bag), gets tossed out the window along with the dying remnants of your low self-esteem.

My son, as I did, quickly learned that, aside from the bus driver's lap, the Bermuda Triangle is by far the safest place to be. The only other safe option is to walk home.

I can clearly remember the horror of once, accidentally, ending up at the back of the bus housing the future serial killers, who, while everyone else was doing homework or watching *The Partridge Family*, would be out mindlessly stomping on snails or plucking the wings off butterflies. I got teased, slapped and spat on simply for being the wrong person in the wrong place at the wrong time.

Normally it's impossible to get past the gatekeepers preventing entry to the inner sanctum of the back of the bus unless the human crush pushes you through. Then, like a dingo caught in a steel trap, you can't escape and this is when you become the snail or the butterfly. Even now there's an invisible force field preventing me from passing a certain point down the bus aisle. If I do, and I've tested this, my blood pressure rises ominously, along with my anxiety levels, and imaginary ants start to crawl along my back.

It's no wonder people don't want to catch public transport anymore which is probably why there are so many traumatised single drivers in cars clogging up the freeways.

Bored and burned-out boys

Life is about doing the ordinary things in an extraordinary way. An example would be my family washing up the dishes in harmony (extraordinary moment in time) without breaking my Royal Doulton over each other's heads (very ordinary behaviour).

Unsupervised, bored teenagers being at home during long, hot school holidays with both parents working full-time spells danger. Toilet paper should only be used in the toilet, deodorant cans are not Darth Vader-style light sabres and matches should not, particularly on a red-hot day, be flicked in the general direction of a pile of dead leaves. Once when I found burned pieces of toilet paper floating around their bedrooms, I told them that 'Toilet paper doesn't grow on trees, you know,' and that if they crossed my line of fire and burned their bridges again, I would pack them off to Nanna's, where they could roast in hell for the rest of the school holidays.

While they didn't exactly volunteer to detoxify their bedrooms or scrape the dried egg snot off the kitchen benches, thanks to the threat of parental spontaneous combustion, their behaviour did improve somewhat.

I don't have the answer to boredom. I can barely relieve my own. We don't have enough money to send them to summer camp and I'm not a one-woman entertainment committee. Once when the holiday budget got blown in one day at the Royal Show, the kids had to amuse themselves in ways that didn't involve the fire brigade getting called to our house every other day.

I eventually fired up their enthusiasm by giving them a recipe book and some hard-earned cash, and convincing them to cook the evening meal. Not only were they relieved of having nothing to do and all day to do it in, I didn't have to cook dinner. If they want to play with fire, let them do so in the kitchen.

I'm not sure why it took a can of whipped cream, some cookie dough, my new sewing scissors and three frying pans for the kids to cook chicken stir-fry for five, but there are some things a parent doesn't need to know. Aside from scorch marks and black soot needing to be scraped off the ceiling and walls, the kitchen was none the worse for wear.

Anyway, it gave me an idea for what to do with them the next time school holidays come around — they can repaint the kitchen. As far as I'm aware, paint is not, in essence, a flammable liquid — unless you add tiresome teenagers and school holidays to the equation.

Jobs for the boys

My two teenage boys, who consider themselves members of Generation Y, now have part-time jobs, working in a butcher's shop and delivering newspapers respectively. They each recently complained to me that they wanted to quit because it's really hard work and people yell at them — and what would I know about back-breaking work sitting at a desk all day?

Back in my day, when Humphrey B Bear and Fat Cat ruled TV and in the years just before Lindy Chamberlain uttered her famous cry 'A dingo took my baby', whingeing and whining were not part of our job description. We worked hard, and when we ran out of jobs to do, washed windows, painted walls and, in miniskirts and high heels, ran errands for the boss and were grateful for the privilege. When we weren't busy, we perfected the art of looking as though we were. Anything was better than being about as useful as a footy player with a hamstring injury during grand final week.

I learned to touch-type at school. The keys were hidden under black tape and a cold-hearted nun rapped my knuckles with a steel-edged ruler every time I made a mistake. It was the era of telex machines, bookkeeping that involved actual books, manual typewriters and the dreaded carbon paper (no convenient 'delete' button). A 'mouse' was still a small, furry creature that cats chased around the garden and spellchecks were done with a book — *The Oxford English Dictionary*. Only Dr Who had liberal access to a computer even if it was the size of Buckingham Palace.

I explained the concept of a manual typewriter to my children but it did not compute. Recently, I saw in a local museum an old Siemens manual telex machine. This, when it was cutting-edge technology, is what I operated in an office in Fremantle in the days *looong* before we won the America's Cup. It was not the buzzing metropolis the shipping port has now become — back then, it was a grey blur in which I used to dodge bullets, knives, broken glass and other people's blood in order to get to work by eight o'clock.

My boys' plan is to sleep in, be chauffeur-driven to jobs as chief executive officers that they will somehow get on the strength of their own ego, and take over the planet before their eighteenth birthdays.

But welcome to the real world, boys! You're not so much Generation Y as Generation Whiners.

Reading kids like a book

Just when you thought it was safe to go back on the internet, yet another holier-than-thou, priggish, tax-payer-funded report tells me what a shoddy job of motherhood I'm doing. Apparently, according to bunch of, no doubt, single, childless researchers with more psychology degrees than can be found in a psychiatric hospital, Smart Kids of Educated Parents Read More Books and Watch Less TV.

It's my experience that you can lead a child to the library but you cannot force him or her to read. Two of my three children rarely read and only one has been overly enthused by Harry Potter, something which I am rather embarrassed to admit. It seems as heretical as being a dedicated pre-primary teacher but confessing under torture that the Wiggles actually make you want to barf up your Fruit Salad, Yummy, Yummy or, to get back to Harry, ditch your Hot Potato, Hot Potato down the bespectacled wizard's dacks.

However, we do own well-thumbed and dog-eared copies of *The Day My Bum Cracked Up* and *The World's Rudest Jokes*, so all is not lost. Apparently, my kids CAN read — they simply choose not to.

Try as I might to bribe, bully, reward or punish my children into the literary life, it just isn't going to happen. In our household, Tim Winton, JK Rowling and Enid Blyton simply can't compete with Foxtel, the internet, PlayStation 3 and Nintendo DS. This is something for which Western Power and battery companies are, I'm sure, extremely grateful, as they would possibly go bankrupt if my kids ever started to read.

According to the latest reports, the news only gets worse if you're a stay-at-home and/or single mother. You are then apparently not only solely responsible for the illiteracy-rate rise, global warming and the near-extinction of the greater-striped Bengal tiger but for the huge ratings of, for example, *The Jerry Springer Show*, which sports such classic episode titles as 'My Transsexual Uncle is now My Daughter's Husband but I'm Having His Baby and She Isn't Happy About It'.

According to my two book-fearing children, you can get a good education watching TV because there's a lot to be learned about life from the goggle box. For instance, you can discover how to form graceful and dignified lasting relationships by watching *How I Met Your Mother* or how to overcome your fear of flying by watching endless repeats of *Air Crash Investigations* while white-knuckling the lounge suite.

I did notice that in this mother-maligning report, as in most government research studies written by male psychologists, the word 'father' is remarkably conspicuous by its absence.

Homework rules

Doing your kids' homework for them is like scrubbing the house just before the cleaner arrives. Satisfying, in a way, but really completely unnecessary.

I once spent many a happy hour on a Grade Two school project competition that involved building a model of Loch Ness, complete with monster made out of plasticine, egg cartons, cotton wool, cardboard, river rocks and garden foliage, and aided by the creative ingenuity that comes from a bottle of Southern Comfort. It started as a joint project but my interfering SmartRider kept insisting on wanting to do stuff himself, so I ended up doing the project secretly after I'd sent him to bed.

I hated school with a passion, preferring to march to the beat of my own drum. Had I been marked on my prowess at Bay City Roller scrapbooking or on my geeky knowledge of the first three *Star Wars* movies, I would have achieved first-class honours.

My kids are now of the age that they don't want a homework-hovering parental. They want a mother who is constantly available but not actually visible. They don't want me choosing their clothes, tidying their rooms or, horror of horrors, turning up at school to speak to their teachers. They're even learning to cook their own dinner, even if I am still expected to do the dishes.

As with medical insurance, they don't need me until they need me. That is, when they run out of money, have an existential girlfriend/boyfriend crisis, or need me to advise them on pimple cream or to provide the perfect alibi to the local constabulary. All three have got part-time jobs without parental input.

My kids call this 'independence' and I call it 'redundancy'. But they're not completely independent yet. While I'm not allowed to enter my younger son's bedroom without permission, I still brush his hair before he goes to school and hitch up his trousers so that his boxers (and bum crack) don't poke out the top. When he's not home, I secretly dust off his Loch Ness Monster project, which, five years on, still sits loudly and proudly on his bedroom shelf.

But, increasingly, rather than feel disenfranchised, I'm moving on, learning to single-task rather than multi-task. I now get to drink cups of hot coffee in the mornings, read the weekend paper without interruption, go on child-free minibreaks to Rottnest, and, to satisfy the homework bug, I've enrolled at university and now have some of my own.

My kids call this 'separating from separation anxiety' and I call it 'getting a life'.

This sporting life

Some people MAKE things happen. Some people stand back and WATCH things happen. And some people sit around and WONDER what just happened.

My husband and I sat back and wondered just what had happened during the AFL grand final. Having actively avoided the TV for most of its duration, parochial guilt finally got the better of us. We reluctantly tuned into the last ten minutes, only to watch the Sydney Swans trounce the West Coast Eagles. Then we puzzled over why the rest of the street in our Perth suburb was yahooing and honking horns in jubilation.

Apparently, we'd somehow tuned into LAST YEAR'S match. I told this to a friend at work, who said, 'Never, ever, EVER tell anyone else that story.'

We'd rather repaint the entire house inside and out, gutters and all, than watch a sporting event on TV — unless, of course, it's *Dancing with the Stars* or, back in the days when it was John McEnroe versus Bjorn Borg, the men's singles finals at Wimbledon. But, as proud parents, we've had to brave many a frosty morning in order to watch our sons and daughter play football and netball.

The last time we watched a footy match was when the Dreamer joined the junior league. This is perhaps the only place where PLAYING the game is far more important than WINNING the game and everyone gets a warm-and-fuzzy-feeling-inducing participation trophy at the end of the season. This is something that certainly prepares children for the real world.

It seems that how to complicate the simple things in life is something that naive children need to learn from an early age. Any parent who has ever scored for their child's t-ball game will know what it's like to sit behind the backstop and take copious cryptic notes, draw diagrams and formulate blueprints on each member's position every time a child strikes the ball from its stationary position. I used to take preventative painkillers whenever it was my turn to score.

What I want to know is, where does all this tedious t-ball tallying go? To the CIA? NASA? Interpol? Or perhaps to the education department, where it's used to formulate school curriculum and policy?

We're not a sporty family. My husband and I are more into elbow-bending a glass of red and page-turning. And, thank goodness, our children appear to be walking — not running, jogging or sprinting — in our footsteps.

Culture clubbed

There's more culture growing on the bottom of our shower curtain, and in the veggie compartment of our fridge, than is present in the hallowed halls of Perth's Cultural Centre.

My family are more used to Hungry Jack's and *Jackass* than we are to peppered tuna salad and Picasso, but in the name of enlightenment, there comes a time when you just have to grit your teeth and drag your kids kicking and screaming into a more refined lifestyle.

My children think that 'refined' refers only to white bread and sugar, 'enlightenment' involves flicking a switch for the PlayStation, 'culture' is what gives yoghurt its unique flavour and 'urbane' is the bloke Nicole Kidman married.

Transcending oneself doesn't involve suddenly deciding to shop at Myer or David Jones instead of at Big W, and just because you've read *The Da Vinci Code*, you can't hang an Arts degree on the wall next to Big Mouth Billy Bass. Speaking of plastic talking fish, a place in which they are strictly prohibited is a museum. This is where, and this is the tricky bit, my kids have to self-oil the rusty hinges of their dormant imaginations. Museums, as well as theatres and art galleries, as I told my culturally challenged teenagers, don't have epilepsy-inducing flashing lights, interactive media and loud explosive noises. The only buttons that might get pressed are the ones belonging to your mother, when you claim to be suffering from excruciating boredom.

Apathy, or is it bloody-mindedness, permeates them when they stay with their grandfather, who's been trying to inject culture, in the form of poetry readings, into them for many years now. But expecting poetry to capture the imagination of computer-hypnotised teenagers is like trying to convince a group of Buddhist monks that dinner with Gordon Ramsay will be an effing great effing spiritual and artistic experience.

The Dreamer wants to go on a mystical journey, but not one that involves meandering around the neural pathways of his mind. He wants to buy a second-hand micro-motorcycle, called a pocket-rocket. I'd rather he traversed the universe of his intellect than zoomed around the streets of our neighbourhood on a dark night at 70 kilometres per hour without headlights, without a helmet and, it would seem, without a pre-frontal cortex.

However, protecting the head involves more than just wearing a helmet. It is also about instilling an intuitive sense of global philosophical awareness of man's inhumanity to man. This is where live theatre, for example, comes into its own. We're taking our daughter to see *Who's Afraid of Virginia Woolf?* But, as I explained to her, it's not just about a typical marriage in which two couples hurl poisonous verbal darts at each other (something she doesn't need to go to the theatre to experience). It's all about exploring the raw, unconscious motives of our deepest, darkest selves, the savage underbelly of why we do the things we do, who we do them to, and why we always hurt the ones we profess to love the most.

My two teenage boys would rather eat dinner off the kitchen floor than pay good money to watch four people get drunk and abusive in the name of art. They'd also rather get down and dirty ice-skating or rollerblading than watch the ballet or go to a Western Australian Symphony Orchestra concert. As a fully paid-up card-carrying member of the Culture Club, it's my job to make sure they know that ballet isn't just about grown men prancing around in groin-hugging lycra, or about marital violence, or over-priced abstract paintings hung in an austere environment, it's really all about life, the universe and the meaning, or lack of it, in our existence.

Bully for you

There are all sorts of people in this world. There are kind, caring and comforting people, and then there those who lack compassion and empathy in any way, shape or form.

In my job (all writers have day jobs) as a receptionist at a public hospital. I come in contact with all sorts of people every day. Some of them must have been kings and queens in a past life, as they demand the royal treatment and throw a two-year-old's tantrum when they don't get it.

So, working in the public trenches of the frontline of humanity means not only occasionally receiving yummy chocolates from grateful people but, every so often, copping abuse from the very people we are trying to help. When I was verbally harassed recently, I said nothing and decided to let karma take its course. I even felt a certain amount of empathy for the harasser because I, too, have demanded the royal treatment on occasion.

On the other hand, I had almost no empathy for the intimidating little sod who threatened to beat up my older son at their high school. My compassion evaporated quicker than red wine at a school reunion, and Mother Power came screaming to the forefront. I rang the deputy principal, who had a quiet, but effective, word in the bully's ear for me.

When she was in primary school, my then six-year-old daughter sat next to a boy, who, for reasons known only to himself, started pinching and punching her. Rather than screaming abuse at his mother, I invited him over for an afternoon play with my daughter, during which he was reasonably well mannered and polite. He never gave her a moment's grief after that, turning his attentions elsewhere.

Two years ago, my oldest son had a full can of Fanta poured over his head by a well-known local bully, and I had a brain snap. Transforming into a lioness protecting her cubs, I burned rubber as I reversed out the driveway, with the other two kids in the back yelling, 'Way to go, Mum!'

With all my children and Fanta Boy's henchmen within earshot, I stood over him blocking out the sunlight, my nose only centimetres from his. I told him, in a surprisingly detached manner, that not only karma would get him if he so much as touched a hair on my son's head.

I believe in karma, that what goes round comes around. It's a very powerful tool. I can look after myself, but if I, their mother, don't look after my children's welfare, who will?

5

Q. How do you survive your family?

A. FOLLOW THE IDIOT'S GUIDE TO THE STOCKHOLM SYNDROME.

Are we there yet?

Travelling with children in a hot car on a long, tedious journey invokes 'the Stockholm Syndrome': that is, a diverse group of individuals forced together by a hostage situation. So, 'the Stockholm Syndrome' is perhaps more commonly known by its other name, 'the Family Outing'.

My husband and I had a particularly bad experience with this on a road trip to Collie a few years ago, on which our three children were locked down in the back of our car for several hours. It's hard to concentrate on a book called *Zen Therapy* with your kids behind you poking, prodding, punching, kicking, burping and farting, and trying to pierce each other's tongues and nether regions with blunt pencils. This is when duct tape and three pairs of handcuffs come in handy.

Things got so bad that at one stage we kicked two of the main offenders, including a child who was at the time choking on a blowfly, out at the bottom of a hill near Harvey and drove off over the horizon with the remaining, well-behaved, kid. Thirty seconds later, excruciating guilt kicked in, badly enough to affect even us. Reluctantly, we drove back, and then rewarded their bad behaviour with lollies and Fanta in an effort to calm them and regain what is oxymoronically known in the parenting industry as 'parental control'.

This is why driving from Perth to Sydney for a family holiday in order to save money on airfares will NEVER be an option. There are families with mythologically well-behaved kids who can make the trip across the Nullarbor together and become bonded tighter than two coats of Weet-Bix to the kitchen ceiling because of it but …

We are not that family.

This is why I'm in favour of Australia adopting China's one-child-policy — I'll certainly vote for the politician who introduces it retrospectively. We recently repeated the trip to Collie, to see Wellington Dam overflow, but this time we took only one child. Bliss. Utter bliss.

Imagine one child instead of three. Only one wet, stinky, mouldy towel to discover under the bed weeks after it was actually used. Only one pair of filthy, smelly shoes outside the front door. Only one child groaning about having to go to school and do homework. What's the sound of one hand clapping in the car on a long road trip? The sound of deafening silence.

It's not about the ball

Some families climb the summits of the highest mountains; sail small boats across the wildest, deepest seas; or ski effortlessly down the steepest slopes the world has to offer. Our family also likes to challenge itself to the fullest — by immersing ourselves in the ageless art of ten-pin bowling.

The sport is not so much about chucking a ball down a laneway as it is about entering into an energetic flow zone without actually having to break into a sweat. And this is very important, because, as a family, we don't do sweat. Unless, of course, it's the small stuff.

Religiously every Thursday morning for many years, I played league bowling with a group of girls. The ecstatic ritual of ball v girl became secondary to having a good, long, hard bitch about friends and family members. Men, mothers and mothers-in-law used to feature prominently (in fact, one of us used to indulge in the fantasy that her mother-in-law's head was the top pin, and would strike out every time). Those were the days when you could smoke inside the venue, drink caffeine and ingest transfat chips, and still think you were getting a healthy dose of exercise, even though your pulse never rose from its ordinary rate.

Through league bowling, I collected (as testimony to my love of the game) a swag of trophies now languishing in the back of a cupboard somewhere in the house. I seem to have passed this love on to my younger son, who I try to take bowling at least once a month.

When I take my children bowling, I have to remind them it's not winning that matters, it's achieving your personal best for your own satisfaction. This is a concept that goes flying out the window every time I play against my husband.

This is when bowling becomes less about getting strikes or spares in a stylish, dignified manner, and more about engaging in a Ben-Hur-style chariot race in which annihilating your soul mate and life partner overrides the actual event. If I remember the rules correctly, ten-pin bowling is a non-contact bloodless sport, unless you're playing against your husband, when it becomes a savage life-or-death battle of the sexes in which there can only be a victorious winner and a worthless loser.

I might be the more experienced bowler but my husband manages to thrash me every time. Or, at least, he thinks he's won — as he does the dishes and iron his shirts for the next two weeks.

Meet the parents

There's only one thing guaranteed to get a teenager's heart rate pumping faster than when a rabid Rottweiler chases you down a blind alley, and that's coming face-to-face with your new girlfriend's parents.

Having anaesthetic-free abdominal surgery, doing ballroom dancing lessons with a broken leg, or crashing your computer and losing three weeks' worth of work isn't nearly as painful as getting scrutinised under the Parental Microscope. This is especially so when the scientists — us — are dissecting the bug — you — on the specimen slide! Our feeling is that if you're man enough to ask our daughter out, you're more than tough enough to have your intentions stretched out on the rack and your ulterior motives firmly squeezed under the thumbscrews.

More than one unsuspecting lad has walked through our front door just as my daughter has run and hid behind it. We, more upright and uptight in our parental duty than Reg Hollis during a union meeting in *The Bill*, surround him and, in authoritarian voices, read him the Miranda warning.

He thought he was taking a new squeeze out for some dinner, a movie and, if he's lucky, a bit of snogging (or worse) in the back seat. He squirms in his floor-length black *Matrix*-style suit, takes off his mirrored fluorescent sunglasses and stares down somewhere in the vicinity of his matching mirrored fluorescent platform shoes as we grill him, without mercy, about his education, or lack thereof, and current and future earning capacity, and remind him that even to think about drinking and driving is illegal and that the thought police do actually exist and have the power to arrest him.

This sort of thing is nothing compared with the psychic torture my father subjected me to when I brought my first boyfriend home. My Freud-fixated father insisted that my very stiff-upper-lip British boyfriend, named after a member of the royal family, was in denial about an urgent need to empty his bladder.

'If you need to go to the toilet, it's over there.'

'No thanks. I'm OK.

'Don't hesitate. You can just go without asking.'

'No thank you, I don't want to go.'

'Well, if you do, you don't have to put your hand up at the table.'

'I'll bear that in mind, but I don't actually want to go!'

'Yes, well, when you do want to go, you know, when you get that urge, it's over there. Are you sure you don't want to go?'

The only thing more excruciating than having your father attempt to potty-train someone you wish to impress is your mother singing (out of tune) in the car on the way to a sixteenth birthday party, with all your friends in the back seat and you dying in agony in the front. The trip allowed at least 45 anxiety-filled minutes between Mundaring and Lesmurdie, giving my mother ample opportunity to break into song at the drop of my self-esteem.

There must be some sort of parenting course my mother and father took that taught them how to excel at embarrassing their children. And this skill must have been passed down the family food chain because, according to my daughter, asking her new boyfriend, who's just stepped over the family doorstep for the first time, if he's planning on drinking and driving with her in the car is embarrassing, whereas I see it as responsible parenting.

Some kids do actually get together in spite of their parents. It's only the fear that our daughter's going to marry some drop-kick that makes us quite fearsome at times. But even some of her drop-kick boyfriends have their endearing qualities. It's easy to become quite attached to someone who spends endless time at your house, even if they can be irritating and somewhat invasive. Sometimes the hardest part for a parent is when your child's relationship ends, and he or she and the ex-partner move on with their lives, leaving one suffering from separation anxiety and wondering whatever happened to so-and-so.

For the couple involved, though, there's nothing deader than yesterday's relationship.

Second home

Recently my daughter phoned home — in a hysterical panic. According to the Wild Child, she'd sliced off her thumb while preparing food at the local restaurant at which she works and the amputated digit was nowhere to be found. I screamed back in an effort to calm her down.

When I got in the car to take her to hospital, the petrol gauge sat well below empty. I was unshowered, with no makeup, and decked out in tracky dacks, a Bay City Rollers t-shirt and ugg boots, all dating back to 1976. It was as if the planets had lined up in a conspiracy to let the world know I am really just an unclean, decade-challenged, slothy slob.

It's a mother's prerogative to yell at her injured children for being so stupid — just before dialling triple zero. And most emergencies happen in the middle of the night, especially earaches. What would appear to be a mild, Panadol-relievable irritation during the day turns into a raging life-or-death emergency during the dark hours when the Painstop has run out and all life in the universe shuts down till dawn breaks.

When one of the kids has an injured arm, he or she sits on the edge of their chair at X-ray clinics willing their limb to be broken, not sprained, because then they get to wear a full-on plaster cast instead of a crepe bandage. To them, this is less a device to align and allow a bone to heal than it is a status symbol designed to elicit sympathetic reactions from family, friends and strangers.

The euphoria at the cast very quickly gives over to whining about poor, pitiful them. After all the attention has been graciously received and the novelty has worn off, the cast reverts to its original purpose and starts to itch like hell.

When my daughter broke her arm, she was only two days later back on the PlayStation, thumbs twiddling away merrily and ceaselessly. This was not the case with my younger son, who faithfully wore his cast for the specified full six weeks, right down to the actual time of day the injury had occurred. Not that he's anal retentive or anything.

Meanwhile, back at the hospital, my daughter's digit was still attached and only a flesh wound had been sustained. She got tea and sympathy, and a bandage up to her elbow, whereas I thought a bandaid, a kick up the backside and a stern lecture on the careful use of sharp knives would have been far more beneficial.

Bear facts of life

In our household, 'roughing it' means having run out of extra-soft toilet paper, drinking instant coffee when we're out of percolated, having to sleep on the lounge suite when the grandparents come to stay, or being forced to make school sandwiches out of two-day-old bread.

This is why we're all fascinated with the Discovery Channel's *Man vs. Wild*. This is the show in which Edward 'Bear' Grylls, who is a handsome British ex-SAS trained aristocrat, sort of a refined, Oxford-educated Steve Irwin with a Hugh Grant plummy accent and a non-Hugh Grant buzzcut, parachutes into the world's danger zones. He's out to prove that if you have local knowledge of bush tucker and can rustle up a basic shelter out of bat droppings, mosquito larvae and Spanish moss, you can survive pretty much anywhere in the world if you get lost.

In the comfort of our four-by-two brick and tile, bonded to our overstuffed armchairs and drinking cups of hot, refreshing tea we watch Bear squeeze fresh elephant dung directly into his mouth, for the moisture content. It is either that or die of dehydration under the African midday sun.

There's a delicious irony in watching a toffee-nosed public schoolboy, who, you'd think, would be more at home drinking Earl Grey from Royal Doulton, rip his teeth into raw trout, lizard gizzards and lion leftovers. Here's a man who not only kills his own spiders but eats them as well.

If my family had to survive on our brains and bush skills we'd be dead within hours. If survival techniques were dynamite, we couldn't blow ourselves up. The last time we went camping, we left the streaky bacon at home in favour of the fat and juicy marron we were going to catch in the local river. Seeing as we're the sort of family who can't find fish in the frozen section of the supermarket, we would've starved had not some kind soul taken pity on us and donated a couple of surplus marron from their brimming-over basket.

In one episode, though, it wasn't edible crustaceans our bare-chested hero had to worry about when he was in the Florida Everglades, it was man-eating alligators. In order to cross a reptile-infested river, Bear chose its narrowest, shallowest spot and for an hour watched the surface for telltale bubbles from submerged alligators.

Like Edward Bear, I travel long, dangerous journeys to hostile territories, and do so every day. Fighting the great unwashed platform natives for a seat on the six-thirty train every morning is rather like battling through thick jungle to find an oasis. Only those with the sharpest elbows live to tell the tale.

Now, that's what I call 'survival of the fittest'.

Why not mention the war

World War One started when Archduke Franz Ferdinand was assassinated in Sarajevo. World War Two began when Adolf

Hitler invaded Poland. World War Three broke out when someone left dog food all over the kitchen bench.

In our household, minor bathroom skirmishes escalate into fisticuffs over who squirted toothpaste on the shower curtain. Territorial disputes flare over who farted in the no-man's-land between the two boys' bedrooms, and health-department-approved dinner-table peace talks eventually break down in favour of Thai takeaway eaten silently in front of the blaring TV.

If it feels like I'm living in a war zone, it's because in the house we have too many Generation Ys who think that because they now have part-time jobs, they're exempt from all household duties, including cleaning up after themselves. The moments of high tension this creates is when the bubbling sewer line that runs under the surface of most family dynamics cracks open. But it's not whether families fight, it's how they fight that matters.

There are several precautions to take when a family hurricane is brewing on the horizon. Batten down the hatches, close the windows, secure all loose and dangerous objects, and attempt to leave face slapping, hair pulling, door slamming, screaming and personal insults to the Three Stooges and *Australian Idol* judges.

Now that we've taken all the fun out of it, let's get down to some Rules of Engagement, as every family needs a good battle to clear the air. Never fight in your underwear in the kitchen with the knife drawer open. Don't use language that would make *Californication* look like a church service. Always remember that it's harder to get bloodstains off cream carpet than it is to get it off cream tiles. Always use 'I' statements. Not as in 'I hate you and wish you were dead,' but as in 'I felt hurt and upset when you used my maths assignment to clean the cat sick off the lino.' Sometimes the most satisfying sound in the world is that of a dish smashing, and smart households set aside a range of crockery for this purpose.

While it's easier to break patterned plates than it is to break patterns of behaviour, there are some families who smugly claim they have never had a cross word or argument with each other, let alone a food fight.

If only they knew what they're missing out on.

It's life, but not as we know it

After watching the exploits and antics on *Big Brother* and *Lost*, I decided to reread William Golding's *Lord of the Flies*, in which civilisation, as a group of unsuspecting schoolboys in an isolated situation learn first-hand, breaks down without adult supervision. This is not unlike the scenarios in our household during school holidays — whether I'm home or not.

The place where law and order really becomes unlawful and disorderly is at the kids' end of the universe. So much so that I thought I'd stumbled onto a crime scene on one occasion that I went to clean their bathroom. As a working mum, I try to turn a blind eye to the sliding gateway leading to where 'The Others' live, and had done so for several weeks. But there does come a time when even Pandora has to open her box.

It wasn't just despair, sorrow, disease and destruction that greeted me as I opened the door. It was a flurry of forensic evidence; a furore of hair, long, short, dog and cat. In fact, there were more discarded tresses on their bathroom floor than in *Hair* the musical.

I also found blood-stained bandaids, scabs, cotton-wool buds with enough wax on them to make several candles, and budding new life forms growing on the soap in the shower recess. Hanging in the air, like a pregnant cloud, was the all-pervading stench of the collapse of familial society as we know it.

It would appear that, in the absence of motherly supervision, my daughter had been testing out her makeup skills on the bathroom walls. Not only did this give Mr Muscle a severe case of lactic acidosis, I discovered that even dynamite couldn't shift the stain. But it was really the toothpaste spitballs on the back of the bathroom door that made me understand that in an adult-free environment, children revert to a primitive state quicker than does a bunch of politicians during question time.

In the middle of all this chaos was The Lord of the Flies itself — a smelly rubbish bin overflowing with the hubris and debris of teenage bathroom life, complete with small flies zooming desperately around the rim in a stubborn and mindless holding pattern. It was the same sort of senile circling motion that bears an uncanny resemblance to my everyday life.

Big Brother isn't just a once high-rating reality TV program with badly behaved participants, it's a concept that lives and breathes fire and smoke in our household during the life sentence known as the School Holidays.

An uplifting experience

It's my belief that most women, be they free-thinking or severely oppressed, old or young, black or white, working full-time or stay-at-home mothers, crave, not expensive new lounge suites, washing machines or ironing boards, but cheap and cheerful peace and quiet.

But rather than committing horrendous crimes for which punishment is six months in solitary confinement (like, say, fraternising with known terrorist organisations or making polony and tomato sauce sandwiches for your child's school lunchbox), occasionally, like Greta Garbo, we just want to be left alone. I've often envied Mary Ann from *Gilligan's Island* for getting marooned long enough to write the definitive recipe for coconut cream pie. But be careful what you wish for, you might just get it.

Of late, I served some time in solitude when I got stuck in a dark and manky lift. But, rather than falling into a sweaty, panic-stricken heap on the torn linoleum floor, deciding which of my children was worthy to inherit my priceless collection of *Planet of the Apes* videos, Princess Di photographs, Electric Light Orchestra LPs, Les McKeown-autographed tartan scarves, and David Cassidy's drummer's drumstick, which I cleverly caught at his 2002 concert, I closed my eyes and took several long, deep, relaxing breaths, just as my therapist had taught me.

My most heart-attack-inducing, scariest, sweatiest, wake-up-screaming-in-the-middle-of-the-night dream involves getting caught in a recalcitrant lift, in which not even the thought of me and Keanu Reeves' entwined in heavy breathing, perspiring bodies and confined spaces could thrill me. Because, as we all know, thanks to the *Speed* movie, being trapped in an elevator involves it dropping a long way and having 20 seconds of life as you know it left to live. The most normally steadfast lift will automatically plummet to earth and waiting at the bottom of the shaft will be huge, jagged metal spikes that have your name engraved on each of them and are guaranteed to skewer you up the jacksy like you're a beef kebab.

But, managing to repress the idea that I was teetering on the precipice of doom, I pulled my aging, creaking body into the lotus position, summonsed all my meditation and relaxation powers, and started chanting 'Ooom, Ooom' in order to quell the rising panic.

This was until I realised that this was the solitude I had been craving at last. No-one could reach me, by any mode of communication, not my skanky teenagers, who wear their clothes for three weeks in a row, or my demanding boss or my domestically helpless husband, who can annoy me just by breathing. There were no epic emails requiring thoughtful responses or cryptic text messages needing replies. No-one could ring to tell me about home-alone siblings and sharp knives, car prangs involving rear-ended police vehicles and extremely angry policemen, or huge mobile phone bills racked up by my daughter.

All of a sudden, rather than feeling that I would be fast-tracked to hell via a stifling steel-grey coffin, I had my own personal living space.

It's not often that mothers are absolutely uncontactable, unequivocally unavailable, both emotionally and physically. The last time I was, I was by myself on a coach heading towards the pointy end of Scotland. No-one knew where I was, because I'd changed my travel plans at the last minute without informing my immediate family back in Australia. I would look into my purse at photos of vaguely familiar people who looked longingly back at me.

I often wondered if the castaways on *Gilligan's Island* had been rescued, would they have hankered after their own particular brand of Paradise Found? I've decided that not only would they pray for another shipwreck, they would actively make one happen.

Driving me crazy

Apparently, there's something more stressful than coming across a booze bus on a Saturday night, and that — according to our neighbour — is your teenage son or daughter getting their driver's licence.

My mother can attest to this. The night I got my hard-earned licence, I borrowed her Toyota Corolla and a parked car jumped out and hit me. I drove off in sheer panic, leaving a smashed headlight, some paint damage and no forwarding address.

Which reminded me of the time when the Wild Child was eligible to attempt to gain some legal 'driving skills' — an oxymoron, where teenagers are concerned — in order to drive me up the wall and around the bend. Mind you, she does that now, without the aid of a motor vehicle.

While she becomes increasingly obsessed with cars, her younger brother the SmartRider and I have become increasingly obsessed with the Perth public train system. Self-confessed trainspotters, we can often be found riding in the carriages between Clarkson, Midland, Armadale and Fremantle (that is, when we're not looking up Transperth websites). This isn't because we have business in these suburbs but just for the sheer joy of riding in a nice clean train gently pootling along the great railway track of life. So nice and clean, that they still have the 'new furniture smell'.

It's a great way to bond with your child, and if the train's crowded enough, you have a legitimate excuse for your offspring to sit on your lap for an extended period of time.

Another bonding experience — as my mother can again attest — occurs when parents try to save money by teaching their teenagers how to drive. My mother and I lasted half an hour before she reached for the Valium. Forking out for expensive lessons was definitely the easier, safer and probably cheaper option.

It's easier finding a seat on an early-morning commuter train than it is staying calm while teaching teenagers anything. And if it's hard staying calm and in control when your non-driver's-licensed kids are out way past their curfew, it's nothing compared with the nervous breakdown to come on a Friday night when your children disappear in a cloud of smoke in their turbo-charged V8 commodore.

Unless you want them to catch public transport for the rest of their lives, it's time to increase your health insurance, fasten your seatbelt as tightly as possible and be prepared for the bumpy road ahead.

Big mother

Synchronicity is when two events occur almost simultaneously in a relevant, purposeful manner. This is rather like when a bunch of Mormons or Jehovah's Witnesses knock on your front door, you hide in a cupboard pretending you're not home, and, a split second later, a bolt of lightning strikes your beloved Barina, which explodes in a brilliant flash of white light and gets rapidly sucked skywards through the smoky updraft of a whirling vortex, never to be seen again. In the synchronistic world, this would be known as a meaningful coincidence.

Our younger son wasn't going to be home for an episode of *Big Brother* 2008 one night because he was shopping for clothes with his father, so he wrote me a two-page, block-lettered, bullet-pointed list on how to press the record button on the VCR. In case I misunderstood his instructions, I had to repeat them aloud before he would leave the house.

He then rang me from the shops because he simply didn't trust Big Mother to record Big Brother.

Our fairly new TV has always been as reassuring as going to a motel and finding a Gideon's bible in the bedside drawer. When a bolt of lightning, in the shape of 'This show is cancelled due to technical difficulties beyond our control' blasted our TV half-way through the recording, it would have been at about the same time our peace-loving, animal rights activist, vegetarian Buddhist ended his call to me, and was embarrassing his father by throwing a public spazz attack over the abundance of leather belts and genuine-leather-upper shoes and the severe lack of non-leather ones. A random coincidence? I don't think so. The gods conspired that night to teach my little control freak a valuable lesson.

There's a place in the universe of your mind in which the deepest, darkest matter resides. Psychologists, neuroscientists and philosophers have been engaging in mental fisticuffs with each other for eons about whether this matter, otherwise known as the unconscious, could possibly be responsible for manipulating events outside human beings', and television network bosses', control. Mothers, of course, have known of the existence of this for many centuries.

That night the tentacles of my well-developed dark matter synchronised with his dark matter and that was when the TV fritzed. If you've ever seen what a drop of water does when dropped onto a hot frying pan, you would have a fair idea of what my little ray of sunshine looked like upon discovering Big Brother had slammed the front door shut in his face.

While I can't quite bend spoons, make objects fly around the room or levitate small animals, if I stare at the back of my son's head for long enough I can make it itch ferociously, so he's very wary of my awesome maternal powers. Even when, in 2020, full-sized holographic replicas of the newly resurrected Big Brother house and inmates have taken up serious space in every living room in Australia, he will never be able to relieve himself fully of an innate suspicion that somehow I was solely responsible for ruining his life that night.

To sleep, perchance to dream

'To sleep, perchance to dream,' cried William Shakespeare's Hamlet, over 400 years before controlled crying and child psychologists became the saviour of many a sleep-deprived mother. But what would a male playwright and poet, living in London away from his Stratford-residing wife and children and getting a full night's uninterrupted sleep, really know about the horrors of sleep deprivation?

Eight hours a night shut-eye is something most mothers can only perchance to dream about. Sleep deprivation is a form of torture by which victims are forced to stay awake for days, or weeks, on end. Upon finally being allowed to fall asleep, they are suddenly awakened and questioned. New mothers are awoken in the middle of the night not by the Russian KGB, sadistic Guantanamo Bay guards or coalition forces in Afghanistan, but by glassy-eyed toddlers who shake and wake them simply to ask if they've fallen asleep yet.

After you've peeled yourself off the ceiling, put Junior back to bed and crawled between the sheets, it can take another three hours before you're relaxed enough to drift off. In the meantime, the newborn has needed to be fed three times, and the cat has been let in and out twice.

For me, being up with the baby wasn't the challenge, it was getting back to sleep. I would lie there desperately counting sheep and avoiding the urge to whack my snoring husband with a pillow. Occasionally I'd jab him in the ribs, not so much because his snoring was loud and intrusive, but because I couldn't bear for him to be fast asleep while I was wide awake. It just wasn't fair.

But if life were an even playing field, my husband and I would have gotten a good night's sleep the time my mother took our two children off our hands so that we could go out to dinner, get reacquainted, make baby number three and, of course, get a good night's sleep. However, in the tradition of the best laid plans of mice, men and exhausted parents, excessive consumption of MSG-laden Chinese food and red wine contributed to us laying awake wide eyed and bushy tailed till dawn, when we managed approximately three minutes' sleep before having to go pick up the kids.

Children are cuddly bundles of genetic material cleverly designed to rob us of every faculty we possess and, in return, nature has decreed we love and cherish each and every one. But most of us would give up the left side of our brain for just one night's sleep.

Severe sleep deprivation can lead to hallucinations, as I found out when my husband and I had tickets to see Tina Turner when my breast-fed son was eight weeks old. I was enjoying the show, cheering and clapping loudly, when my husband pointed out to me that she hadn't actually come on stage yet. I was apparently giving a standing ovation to the soundcheck man and to the road crew setting up the speakers.

Sleep deprivation can, indeed, manifest itself as temporary loss of contact with reality. One afternoon when both my baby and toddler were fast asleep, I was, although exhausted, watching *Rambo: First Blood*, propping up my eyelids with toothpicks every time they started to droop. I should have been asleep but was afraid of missing out on something, quietly going mad in a way that not even the Bard could imagine. Just as the credits started to roll, the children woke up and began to cry. In the padded armchair by the TV, no-one can hear you scream.

Like the persecuted Vietnam vet I was watching, I felt alone, confused and overwrought. I just wanted to run and hide but the psychic umbilical cord that tied me to my children wouldn't let me. This is the same bond that had me pushing a pram up and down the hallway for hours on end every night trying to change my night-owl baby into a normal day bird.

According to the playgroup police, what my family needed was a strict routine. However, ordinary events happening at the same time every day in an organised fashion at our place was about as likely as Oprah Winfrey marrying the long-suffering and largely absent Stedman.

Before I had children, I worked full-time, studied part-time and did volunteer work, as well as having an immaculate house and garden. I was secretly contemptuous of people (especially mothers) who couldn't get their shit together. My life centred around lists — lots of them, carefully worded, neatly written and symmetrically magnetised to the fridge. Each weekend, my husband and I would methodically work our way down the list of jobs. I was the Squeaky Clean Uber-Queen of Meticulous Routine.

Nine months later, I went from vain to insane, as my kingdom was ruthlessly toppled by treasonous infants hell-bent on overthrowing the reigning monarchy. Routine and sleep, like expensive restaurant dining and uninterrupted sex, went right out the Wiggles-curtained window.

Time is really the only answer to child-induced sleep deprivation. Little people do turn into teenagers for whom getting out of bed is just as difficult as getting them into bed. Our Shakespearean Tragedy of Tiredness has turned into *Dawn of the* (living) *Dead* because, at the weekend, none of our children get up till the crack of lunchtime.

6

Q. Shrink-wrapped on the other side of the couch and wondering who to blame?

A. MUST BE YOUR MOTHER, YOUR THERAPIST ... OR YOURSELF.

I'm listening

Some people are born with a silver spoon in their mouth, while others scoot down the birth canal with their size elevens firmly wedged between their nose and chin.

Personally, I like to wear my favourite flatties between my lips because that way there's no room for me to say anything I am sure to regret. Plus, a full mouth which cannot speak can mean a pair of ears that are not only listening intently but, in a very astute and meaningful manner, progressively learning.

My psychotherapist, whose flatties are firmly planted on solid ground, has been listening and learning very carefully for several years now. To her credit, never once have I seen her stifle a well-earned yawn, watched in dismay as her eyes glazed over or seen her slowly fall to one side, suffering from stultifying sleep-inducing boredom, as I tell the same old story over and over and over and over again.

She's done such a good job on me that I now find myself wanting to study and collect books on psychoanalytic psychotherapy pretty much the same way Angelina Jolie collects other people's husbands and overseas-based orphans.

Psychotherapy is all about active listening, and active listening is inherently exhausting. So is trying to promote and sell the 'open ears, shut mouth' concept to a household of strongly opinionated males who start every other sentence with 'Just listen to ME ...' accompanied by aggressive finger poking in the general direction of the errantly perceived non-listening party.

Enduring long, pointless arguments is part and parcel of parenting teenagers. Taking a leaf out of my therapist's book, I close my mouth, open my ears, and let them rant and rave about what ails them at this particular point in time and space, without interjecting with:

'What you SHOULD do is this ...' or

'What you MUSTN'T do is that ...'

My parents once said of my younger sister that if she would only listen to what they had to say, she would never make any mistakes.

Boys and their fathers can argue loudly and incessantly about who's not listening the most but I was rather taken aback, and secretly thrilled, to hear my teenage son say to my husband, during a very recent argument, that 'YOU never listen to me, but Mum always does.'

Looks like I might have a career in psychotherapy after all, and I should be qualified to practise just in time to help my beleaguered progeny recover from the trauma of their own tortured upbringing.

Parental power struggle

According to Therapy World, there's a phenomenon called 'transference'. This is when you relate to other people, especially therapists, through the murky, distorting lens of repressed childhood experience.

That is, psychologists believe that current events in your life are hard-wired by how your parents dragged you up, kicking and screaming, from the womb to the tomb. There's negative, positive, idealising and devaluing transference, and, if you stay in therapy long enough, you not only get to experience them all — sometimes in one session — but you can also end up having more issues with your therapist than you do with your parents.

Being an adult guest in my parents' home evokes all sorts of transferences. A year or so ago I stayed overnight with them. In the morning I decided to boil an egg for breakfast, whereby my father subsequently knocked over expensive antique furniture in his paternal fervour to inform my inadequate self that I was doing it all wrong. I needed to do it the right way. His way.

Apparently, I can't cook an egg to save my life. I can whip up a three-course gourmet dinner for ten, but boiling something that comes from a chook's bum requires the exasperated intervention of Dear Old Dad.

No wonder therapy appears the fastest growing industry in the world.

I stayed overnight there again when I dropped the boys off for the last week of the school holidays. We went for a walk to the local shops and I informed Dad that I wanted to buy some ice-cream. He told me I couldn't have any. According to Dad, I'm never too old be under his callused parental thumb.

I told him that, given my age, he had no control over whether I bought ice-cream, be it banana-ripple or bubble-gum flavoured, even if it was minus five degrees outside and several brass monkeys were in severe distress. I think I may even have stamped my foot for emphasis.

Later, as I served up my illicit bounty, he retaliated in an immature way by putting the needle on *Dean Martin's Greatest Hits* and playing it at full volume, rather like the way I disturb my children's sensibilities by blasting out Suzi Quatro's or The Sweet's *Greatest Hits* (they run out of the room, ears bleeding, screaming in agony. I often wonder what they will be telling *their* therapist in ten years' time.)

You can choose your therapist, but you can't choose your family.

Privatising my privates

I have read that Angelina Jolie and Brad Pitt wanted to thank the world for respecting their privacy during the birth of their twins.

Privacy!! Last time I looked, there was nothing private about giving birth, no matter who you are or how much money you put into the coffers of a third-world country or a hospital on the French Riviera. Having a baby is the most spectacular display of Privates on Parade since Pammy and Tommy did the wildest thing on a boat.

Private health cover has nothing to do with covering your privates so that you're not embarrassed and everything to do with paying exorbitant gap fees so you can be advised by a, no doubt, single and child-free student doctor to stick your feet into those innocuous-looking instruments of torture otherwise known as 'the stirrups'.

And, while you're lying there with your ankles decorating your ears, could you just scoot your bottom a little further down the table, please? This unique little pozzy is usually reserved for yogi masters, unpregnant men who manage to look serenely dignified while in excruciating pain.

Never use the words 'dignity' and 'stirrups' in the same sentence unless you are talking about lack thereof. Thank heaven prostate tests were invented — there is a god, after all.

And not that Angelina, she of the child-bearing lips, had to scoot her pert little bum down the operating table. According to media reports, she had a caesarean. As we mothers of unnaturally born children have always been told, dodging a vaginal birth, regardless of the medical reasons, is like going back to work and putting your kids in child care. Not only is it a lifestyle cop-out but it's acting like a selfish mother-faker, to boot.

Privacy is always in short supply when your kids grow up. My two boys violate the Geneva Conventions Bill of Human Rights far more often than the prison guards at Guantanamo Bay do. This is especially when, armed with a video camera, they barge in on me while I'm having a long hot shower and defoliating, wearing nothing but shaving cream on my legs. Luckily, I managed to erase the tape before it ended up on YouTube.

Expecting my kids to respect my personal space and right to privacy, even if their pocket money, and sometimes life, depends on it, is like feeding them baked beans for breakfast and expecting them not to pass wind in an exuberant fashion for the rest of the day.

Brad and Angelina may be able to run and hide from the paparazzi, but, as they'll find out over time, there just aren't enough hiding places in the world to escape from their ever-increasing intruding offspring.

Existential terror

Some people live their lives in quiet desperation. The rest of us conduct our business desperately, in a loud and vulgar manner. I have a sneaking suspicion that most people I know think that my life is a window-shattering, abrasively uncouth hissy-fit just waiting to happen.

And they may well be correct. Not long ago, I was driving my children to school when I had a moment of sheer existential terror. The front windscreen cracked in several places as a result of frightening thoughts simultaneously invading my brain with ear-splitting clarity but I decided to postpone my hissy fit till I'd locked the kids out of the car first.

Not only had I forgotten to sew a button on my husband's work shirt but I'd also failed to pack my son a fat-free lunch and, sandwiched in between, there was the realisation that one day I was going to die and possibly not from old age (either that or a Veronica's song had just come on the radio).

But moments of age-related terror are not only part and parcel of menopausal angst. When my SmartRider son didn't want to get a year older, he came to me wanting to know if there was anything I could do about it.

He was still at the age when he thought his mother could perform miracles. (As far as I'm aware, the only supernatural occurrence that has ever happened in our household is when I manage to get out of bed before 10 am on a shivery Sunday morning.)

So, I asked him, whose favourite song was Youth Group's 'Forever Young', that if I could turn back time, did he really think I'd be turning 48 the next year?

On a cognitive level, I understand that staying forever young is not on my options menu, but growing old disgracefully definitely is. Something I manage to do very disgracefully is housework, which I believe is a common cause of wrinkles. When I'm scrubbing the kitchen floor to perfection, I'm concentrating so hard on getting the grit out of the lino grooves that I've got furrows in my forehead deep enough to hide the entire contents of Kate Moss's bathroom cabinet in.

Although I must confess that in the past I've been known to hold the baby in one hand and a bottle of vod — I mean, washing-up liquid, in the other, and without spilling a single drop, I might add.

If someone else does the dirty work, I don't get the wrinkles. A win-win situation for me, because the worst thing anything could write on my epitaph would be 'She died with a dishcloth in her hands'.

'She died with a glass of vodka in her hands', is, however, perfectly acceptable.

Garden state

There's something about gardening that's pleasant and relaxing, and it gives the soul a gentle workout that inspires creativity. Or perhaps it's just that bougainvilleas, hydrangeas and daffodils don't answer back when you lecture them. You can bend and break plants to your will, and they won't get all mouthy and opinionated or kick you in the shins. But my garden, as do my children, sometimes leads me to that fine line between pleasure and pain.

Children are like cocos palms, diosmas and weeds — they thrive in the most barren places and can endure endless bad karma. Even when deprived of adequate sunshine, kindness and attention, they seem to flourish madly, growing tall, healthy and strong — and, by doing so, flip me the finger every time I look at them.

I can throw handfuls of fertiliser at my roses, gently prune their branches and whisper sweet nothings into their delicate buds — and then the buggers wither and die on me. Maybe I should treat them with the same disdain that I do my children. Then I'd have a garden full of fragrant flowers blooming against all the odds.

Before we had children, our front garden was immaculate. Weeds were pulled out of the ground before they were actually visible to the naked eye. The brick paving was spotless, and the grass was definitely greener on our side of the fence. And then I got pregnant.

I have precious photo albums full of pictures of our garden at varying stages, from birth till now. In them, bluebells, tulips and freesias erupt through the ground like Baby's first tooth. But now my garden, like myself, is approaching its menopausal years and nothing short of a bulldozer and facelift will bring it back to its former glory.

One only has to take a look at someone else's front garden to get enormous insight into family life beyond the front door. If boring people have immaculate gardens, we must be one very exciting family indeed. Of course it doesn't help when your boys go round the garden with a baseball bat beheading all the agapanthus flowers, and doing what boys, and men, do best, that is, treating the Great Outdoors as one big urinal.

Raising well-balanced, shiny happy people is about as easy as growing vegetables in the middle of Australia. But, somehow, with very little effort on my part, I've managed to grow three robust potato couches right in the middle of my lounge room.

Mirror, mirror on the wall, who reflects you most of all?

I've often suspected that my children don't listen to a word I say. But if that's the case, how come they never fail, usually in a very public place, to repeat verbatim my words in all their glory?

One day when my daughter was two, I was rushing in from the car because the phone was ringing. I couldn't quite get the key in the front door lock and so I let rip some very choice language. For the next three weeks, she went around the house saying, 'futting hett' every time something thwarted her, which, as a two year old, was anything and everything she came in contact with. The more I told her not to say it, the more she repeated it, and for a while I got some very stern looks from total strangers in the local supermarket.

Children are little mirror images of their parents. If you want to know what's going on in someone else's house, just listen to and observe the behaviour of the small and the not-so-small children, and then watch the parents, especially the mother. Mothers, it would seem, have far more influence over their children than Facebook, *Top Gear* or Habbo Castle ever will.

So, when kids get angry and thump the computer keyboard, get loud and argumentative with shop assistants, or backchat the bus driver, who are they emulating? Chances are, it's the mother, the same person who cringes with despair when her children are rude, but is also the person who should take the credit when her children are kind to animals, stand up for older people on public transport or commit some other random act of consideration.

There's so much pain and anguish involved both in being and having a mother. We look through a glass darkly, into a distorted mirror, at our feminine and nurturing selves. I relentlessly measure my children's behaviour against my parenting skills, pretty much always taking the blame for the bad behaviour and attributing the good behaviour to random luck. I can be the fall guy for my offsprings' bad manners but act surprised when told at a restaurant that my three teenagers are well behaved.

Kids mimic their parents in many ways other than verbally. I recognise the selfishness of the young in my daughter, and the unadulterated youthful laziness of not wanting to lift a finger around the house in my sons. I was no different at their age.

It's been my experience that while children ape parental behaviour pretty much subconsciously, there are some things that seem to be innate and so completely beyond anyone's control. Tall, slim parents who adore sport seem to produce tall, slim children who are also physically active, and plump, armchair-hugging, book-loving, glasses-wearing parents appear to create children who also prefer reading to exercise.

No matter how much you love your parents or how wonderful you think they are, it can make your skin crawl with imaginary ants when you hear yourself talking to your children, or your husband, with the same tone and inflection that your mother did to you. If my husband ever wants to incur my wrath, he just has to utter the classic line, 'You sound just like your mother!'

Of all the disturbingly familiar moments that stir up the many anxious emotions that accompany motherhood and make one shudder inwardly, there are very few that are on par with hearing the ghost of your mother's voice in your own, or your own voice from within your daughter, or seeing your features reflected in your son's face. I watch the SmartRider's snub nose flare in hot temper the same way mine does, and in the same way my father's did as well. My boys each have two semi-visible half-eyebrows, just like I do. And my daughter has tight, spiral curls, just like her father's, which are the reason why she straightens her hair every day. Looking like your parents is both reassuring and bothersome. I might think my parents are attractive, but I don't want to see their face when I look in the mirror.

Your children are a mirror to your soul, which is not always a good thing. They can, after all, echo your own narcissism and bad behaviour and not necessarily conform to the wholesome and respectful image you would like portrayed publicly. You know instinctively, even if you don't like it, that they have reflected you accurately, warts and all, in their words, images and actions. It's not the most comfortable feeling in the world.

When I want my kids to behave, I have to be a good role model. If I want them to do the dishes properly, without complaining, I have to help them do the dishes. If I want them not to speak angrily, I have to control my temper as well. Do as I do, as well as what I say.

Most kids seem to have a built-in desire to copy their parents in order to become the best person they can be, but, if boys often want to be like their fathers, some girls will do anything to be as different from their mothers as possible. Only with age comes the wisdom to realise that your mother wasn't as bad as you thought she was, and that she and your father did the very best job they could, even if you thought at the time that they should have been sacked.

There is nothing on earth that stirs our subconscious, our dreams and ambitions, our deep, deep yearnings and desires, more than seeing our physical features in someone we gave birth to, and knowing that it will most likely be passed down for generations to come.

This quest for immortality, trekking the Holy Grail of existence, is what keeps humanity reproducing itself. We want and need to leave behind a legacy to prove that we once existed, and the way most of us do this is to leave behind little replicants of personal timelessness.

If children are a work of art in progress, parents are the artists who wield the paintbrush, apply the many strokes, and choose and fashion the myriad colours and tones in order to produce their own particular masterpiece that will, hopefully, survive long after their own preordained end.

Near-life experiences

Life is an experience, a journey that is sometimes without a clear path or destination. At least, that's what I told myself in heavy traffic on the way to work, when I had a spiritual epiphany. However, unlike the star of *Mad Max*, this was without the aid of an open bottle of tequila in the car and a booze bus looming on the horizon. This involved my teenage daughter and her friends.

I decided I love being around teenagers. Listening to their brutally honest assessments might not make for pretty conversation but since when was life v. pretty? Life is v. messy. But out of the Chaos Theory that abounds in most households, certain patterns of behaviour evolve. So, if we dig deep enough into our past, we can actually remember what it was like to be young.

Not so long ago, sitting around the table on a Friday, I had a rebirthing experience with my daughter and her friends. We discussed life, the universe, other children's parents, fear and loathing, drugs and alcohol, pizza toppings, self-harm, suicide and why *Stars Wars* is better than *Lord of the Rings*. Mothers are the teachers of the universe, being mentors, psychologists and spiritual guides. It's our job to transform our grotty little offspring into civilised human beings.

It's not only teenagers who suffer from growing pains — I've had my fair share of menopausal angst. The feelings are the same as I had back then, they're just separated by 30 years. Although my children have told me that my teenage experiences were so long ago as to be totally irrelevant to them, eventually they conceded that perhaps the person who hangs their undies out on the line might be of some spiritual significance after all.

I've been trying to teach my boys about ancient wisdoms embodying the ecstatic benefits of spiritual enlightenment. But it's rather difficult to teach this to two hormonal teenagers intent on beating each other's brains out over who scarfed down the last piece of meat lover's pizza.

Actually, boys, it was me.

Even mothers need mentors and spiritual guides, older women who have been there before. It's my experience that there's a network of wise old crones out there teaching mothers about motherhood, teaching which does not necessarily involve nappies, bottles and what sort of cake to bake for the school fundraising stall. It's more about tapping into your divine potential by quelling insidious fears that life is just all too hard.

Most teenagers and some adults, including the star of *Lethal Weapon* and *Braveheart*, think it's all about them. But it isn't, it's all about everyone — and everything — that's ever inhabited this wonderful life-giving planet of ours.

Older, not necessarily wiser

Last month I turned on the TV, sat down to watch *The Poseidon Adventure*, and decided that I really must be getting older because Shelley Winters didn't seem all that ancient, like she did when I was ten years old and it was 1972. Instead, my 47-year-old self thought she was rather buxom, and alluring for her age.

Watching reruns of *Gilligan's Island* proves even more alarming. Back in the seventies, I had a crush on Gilligan. In the eighties, I had the hots for the Professor, and in the nineties I was thinking that the Skipper wasn't all that bad looking either. If ever I start having wild sexual fantasies involving Mr Howell, I'll be sublimating my libido by booking my crotchety self into a retirement home and passing the time knitting blanket squares or, worse still, baby bootees.

Not that there's any danger of becoming a grandmother next week, or the week after that. My daughter wants a career, a car and chance to cruise around the world for a few years. In that order. She doesn't want kids. Can't think why!

God, I envy her on that account. I wouldn't give my kids up for the world but sometimes I feel duped by evolution, biology and the passing years. Who would I be without my children? How would I define myself? *Sliding Doors*, and all that.

Recently I was at the local hairdresser's, minding my own business, when I saw the reflection of a young girl in the mirror opposite, and my first thought was that she looked like I did at sixteen.

Slowly, it dawned on me that it WAS me. Well, actually, my daughter, who had come in, unbeknownst to me, for a spur-of-the-moment haircut. It was a poignant Minties Moment that made me want to eat a whole bag of them.

I looked at my beautiful daughter — my nemesis, my doppelganger, my 'through a glass darkly' mirror image, with her long, thick un-grey hair, and clear skin smoother than Lindt chocolate. I was gazing enviously down the corridor of time to when my life was smaller, easier and simpler; when the block-of-flats-sized mental baggage I now carry around was only the size of small brick.

Growing old is compulsory but growing up is, well, optional. But, in any case, it's not the thought of wrinkles, Alzheimer's, rheumatoid arthritis or Zimmer Frames that disturbs me. Again, it's the thought that I might one day find myself having long, languorous fantasies about Thurston Howell III, a teddy bear, a thatched bed and a deserted island.

Entropy therapy

Needing some personal inspiration for peace during a rowdy teenage sleepover at our place, I opened at random a page from my bible, a psychology dictionary, and came across a new word, 'entropy'. It's a psychotherapy term for 'the amount of psychic energy that is no longer available for recycling'. I like to call it

The Law of Diminishing Returns for Working Wives and Mothers.

And, to put it into a psycho-bio-social context, when my husband was gardening recently and stabbed the back of his left hand with a 5 cm Robellini thorn, I had an Existential Entropic Reaction. Mustering up all my available care factor, I said in my tenderest voice, 'Here's 20 cents!'

It's not as though I'm not concerned. I hope his hand's OK, else who's going to finish off the weeding? But my care factor, like the use of his left hand, has temporarily gone AWOL.

Another example of maternal entropy is pulling up in the driveway, seeing my boys' expensive bikes rusting in the pouring rain and thinking, 'How annoying. I've run out of chocolate again.' Or unloading the dishwasher and being oblivious to the heat-hardened food bits glued onto the otherwise clean crockery and happily stacking it back in the cupboard.

But it's not 'dishwasher snot' that gets up my nose as much as the tissue variety that my family spreads around the house like Hansel and Gretel's breadcrumbs. For some reason, they need to leave a trail of thin white tissue paper to locate the TV or fridge from the bedroom or couch.

That's when working full-time is a bonus. Becoming psychically unavailable is about minimising my internal and external life, choosing my arguments, ignoring the conflicting voices in my head, and investing what's left into something I really want to do, such as sleeping, daydreaming or dozing on the train to work. I've finally learned that you can't solve problems or burn up kilojoules mentally fist-fighting invasive circular thoughts or thoughtless teenage children.

Trying to keep tabs on the murky stuff in my kids' heads is rather like trying to drink a bottle of chardonnay while riding a roller-coaster. If you manage to take enough on board, it can really shake you up and down and addle your brain.

This is the sort of hangover that only another glass of wine can cure.

Mindfully mindless

Mindfulness, in the Buddhist sense, involves living in the present and observing all thoughts and emotions that enter your mind without judging them good or bad.

I'm sure that even the Dalai Lama had his own teenage moments before he grew up to be the Chief Executive Officer of Mindfulness and Meditation. I'm, of course, trying to teach my boys to be mindful but they think that, with a surname like Lama, the ex-religious leader of Tibet is some sort of foreign, woolly mountain goat with bad breath and a mindless spitting habit. Attempting to teach them mindfulness is like trying to tune in a TV without an aerial. No matter how hard you try, the reception will pretty much remain grey and fuzzy till they hit, say, 25.

In any case, the big picture of life can be so frighteningly high definition that I like to take the approach that (like rotting gutters, cat hair on the sofa or a Jason Donovan comeback CD) if I don't think about it, it's not happening. If I eat a family block of chocolate and no-one saw me do it, did it really pass my lips?

My kids subscribe to the theory in their way: that is, that if they left their homework diary at school, is their English assignment actually due? If a thirteen year old has an ingrown toenail and begs me not to mention it to the doctor but to write him a note to excuse him from sport for the rest of his life, will the toenail grow out itself?

My mind gets so full that it grows hot and feverish because I think about burning potential issues way too much. That's when the big piece of walnut-covered coffee cake in the kitchen whispers my name and I can't answer it quickly enough. Eating to dull the pain is senseless but, hey, it works! Some of the time.

I've learned over the years to deal with emotions in a mindful manner. To sit with them and observe how I feel in my body. How do I feel within about the rotting gutters? Do I embrace and celebrate the fact that they've lasted 20 years, or do I get wild that my husband hasn't got around to fixing them himself, or do I just hike up the credit limit, consult the *Yellow Pages* and live mindfully ever after? This is the Buddhist equivalent of counting to ten. If you practise for long enough, it becomes second nature.

There are times when I think my kids share this capacity for deep thought. But then ten minutes after a long, deep philosophical discussion about existentialism, I catch them shooting fully loaded stapler guns at each other or holding their grubby fingers over my scented candle flame just to see how long it will take for their finger to light up.

Sometimes, like my boys, we all need to be mindlessly mindless, and there's no better way of doing so than going to the movies and pigging out on popcorn, Coke and ice-cream and not pondering the fact that *Dude, Where's My Car?* has been empirically proven by meta-analytical research to shrink brain cells and considerably decrease one's capacity for introspective thought. It's just as important to be mindless, also known as 'vegging out', as it is to be mindful.

The teenage brain, like teenagers themselves, needs to sleep in till the crack of lunchtime. Now, who wouldn't be mindful doing that occasionally?

Peace be still

There's an old Buddhist piece of wisdom about letting go and emptying one's mind of clutter, so that all suffering will end, and peace and harmony reign forever.

So, I let my husband and two boys go on a long-weekend camping trip. They left the fridge and house empty, thus bringing an end to MY suffering and giving ME peace and harmony.

I spent the time in a cone of internal silence, listening to MY sad, weird, drunk music (which is anything with a synthesiser and without lyrics, according to my children) and without *Video Hits* jack-hammering my brain into mush.

On the Sunday morning, I woke up to the sound of birds singing and, for the first time in ages, didn't want to throw rocks at them. I ate strawberries and chocolate for breakfast; enjoyed a long, leisurely shower; walked around the house sacred and naked; and self-reflected and meditated myself into a blissful state.

When I was out driving for a couple of hours, I was in such a contemplative head space that I didn't hear the car behind me furiously honking its horn, which was followed by my being overtaken by a gorgeous, young blonde woman in an expensive foreign car, angrily flipping her finger at me, while screaming profanities. To my amazement, I didn't react.

I have, in the past, as my children will testify on a stack of Bibles, screamed unspeakable abuse at fellow road users I perceive to have done me wrong. As my daughter once remarked, 'That was way out of proportion to the situation, Mum.'

When I arrived home, I saw that nothing had stirred, not the dirt nor the dust. There was no buzzing, sawing, pounding, rustling, humming or vibrating. No rank testosterone hanging in the air. The cats hadn't moved either, and the atmosphere was as still and silent as my brain cells.

That is, until my daughter came home, and started rocking and rolling about all the injustices, perceived or otherwise, that had happened to her during her day at work.

I don't have a room to call my own and in which to be creative. I share the house, the bathroom, the only computer and desk space with my family. All I have is the space inside my head — a retreat where, if I let go and empty my mind, all outside distractions disappear.

My husband and boys might sometimes be spending the weekend sleeping under a tent in the wilderness, but, at the end of the day, I'm the happy camper.

7

Q. Waves of emotions or tsunamis of guilt?

A. EMO IS NOT A DIRTY WORD.

Domestic hit or miss

I do love my family — my husband, children, parents, in-laws and sister and her fiance — but we tend to be somewhat antagonistic when we get together for dinner. So, it's always a good idea to set the table with Qantas-approved plastic knives and forks.

But the real secret weapon of mass destruction in our house would be my daughter, who works long, hard hours.

At the weekends, when her two noisy brothers accidentally-on-purpose wake her up, she explodes from her bedroom like a cave-dwelling moray-eel, who, upon seeing movement, shoots out and bites the head off passing unsuspecting prey before retreating back into its dark hollow to savour the tasty morsel.

Who needs long-range nuclear missiles when you're living with a fire-breathing teenage terrorist? And, like Amy Winehouse having yet another 'bad reaction to drugs', my two boys never quite learn from their experiences — even though their heads have had to grow back several times recently.

There's an aspect of domestic violence that is largely overlooked by the great unwashed media and which is cheerfully thriving, and not in a terribly healthy way, in our house. This is when my three kids want to beat the living daylights out of each other for major crimes, such as passing in front of the TV when *Girls of the Playboy Mansion* is on, or pilfering from the pantry the last bag of salt and vinegar crisps to munch on during said TV show.

It's me they really should be looking out for, as I won't tolerate bloodshed or brutality in my house, unless I'm the one dishing it out. Verbal violence, however, is up for grabs by anyone in our family who has a pair of vocal cords and wants to make my ears bleed. (There will be significant advantages to slowly going deaf in my old age.) And don't talk to the hand, because it's not listening either. It's too busy smacking the bottom of the child who's trying to bite it off.

I've taken domestic deafness to the level of a fine art. Either that or De-Nile is still the most frequented travel destination for world-weary mothers. If my kids want to act out the World Wide Wrestling Federation the way we used to skip rope and play elastics, who am I to stand in their way? Perhaps there is such a thing as justifiable violence between siblings?

Then my obligation as a resourceful mother would be to provide the boxing ring and gloves, and sit back with a glass of wine and a smug grin — and wait for the games to begin.

Emotional IQ

If you want to change your children's behaviour, or anyone else's, first you have to take a good, hard look at your own set of moral rules.

Children and husbands, and even the family dog, absorb Mother's tumultuous moods via osmosis. As the rage regulator in my household, when I'm angry my family starts bickering and arguing, and then the dog starts to look worried.

But whether you're a housewife peeling vegies for dinner or an astronomer peeling back the outer layers of the universe, you need to develop that happy attitude by which you can just chill out, zone in and let the good vibes flow.

And the good vibes flowed for me the other week as I spent two hours pulling clover and winter grass out of the brick paving, and thus unearthed the hidden Buddha within. As Lance Armstrong the cyclist wrote, 'It's Not About the Bike'. Whether you're parachute jumping out of an aeroplane, mopping tomato sauce (or was it blood) off the kitchen floor, writing the next number-one song or doing a spot of therapeutic gardening, the zen-flow state can be the same.

As I mentioned, my children having built-in radars that pick up and home in on any moods I might be having, means that my behaviour is reflected in theirs. One only has to look at little children's social graces to get a fair idea of what's happening in their particular household.

Emotional IQ has very little to do with Intelligence IQ. You can be the most brilliant gene-splicing, atom-splitting scientist in the world but what does that matter if you go to work grumpy or get home in a foul mood and stir up the rest of the cosmos?

People like that affect other people — just like ripples on a pond or a tidal wave, depending on how good you are at tuning them out and, instead, peacefully focusing on your inner metaphysical life.

The more tranquil I am, the less restless my children become, and when that's the case, my husband, my children's teachers, and the rest of civilisation, are extremely grateful.

Family baggage

Every day on the train there's a bombardment of messages about not leaving unaccompanied luggage behind, just in case it's hiding Osama Bin Laden, Iraqi insurgents, The Chaser boys or Kevin Rudd's long-lost personality.

So, when I discovered a lone suitcase loitering with intent next to a Perth underground railway platform seat, I got very excited and, with trembling hands, dialled triple zero.

More on that later, but suspicious suitcases are not the only unaccompanied baggage that gets freebie rides on the Perth train system. My latch-key SmartRider used to amuse himself by travelling free from Whitfords to Perth after school every day, with the entire fleet of Transperth guards, and his parents, none the wiser.

When the trainspotter wasn't rorting the system, he was riding his bike or rollerblading along the footpath next to the freeway, doing laps of Lake Monger, while I was chained to my desk thinking he was at home safe and sound Googling 'sporting injuries' on YouTube.

It was only when he fell off the bike and broke his arm five suburbs away that I got an inkling of his extracurricular lifestyle. That's when, like a suitcase full of Semtex, I exploded in every direction and gave my injured son the bollocking of a lifetime — as only a terrified, guilt-ridden working mother can.

Keeping your eyeballs firmly glued on several free-range children while grinding away at the workplace requires the agility of a one-eyed, one-armed, double-bladed knife juggler standing on her head while watching a *Malcolm in the Middle* marathon.

Kids somehow survive, despite their parents' best intentions and endless Foxtel sitcoms. Ignorance is bliss. Unadulterated bliss. Until the police, local hospital or truant officer eventually tracks you down at work to please explain. More inexplicable than Kevin Rudderless winning the election is the fact that my family is still here despite some very *I Shouldn't Be Alive* moments.

Ones a bit like the one I thought I was having after ringing the police to report that menacing piece of stand-alone baggage. If you see something, say something, and I saw something and told someone, who, in a very bored voice, thanked me for my concern and hung up.

Therefore, I could only assume that when Perth didn't get blown through the hole in the ozone layer, the al-Qaeda suspect cleverly disguised as a black-and-red suitcase was either retrieved by its unsuspecting owner or secretly imploded by the terrorist police.

Let's hope the same thing doesn't happen to my unescorted SmartRider.

Horror scope

While I was listening to the radio the other morning, I heard an astrologer say, 'Pisces — Your children will enrich your life.'

That afternoon I sent my son out to buy a Lotto ticket and it was when I didn't win a million dollars that I thought that, maybe, my horoscope had been a complete load of bollocks.

Then the penny dropped. Ah! It had meant children would EMOTIONALLY enrich my life in a positive, affirming, warm and fuzzy manner that has absolutely nothing to do with instant financial gain. Double bollocks, I thought.

My emotionally enriching children encroach on my life to the point where I consider myself to be an Emo Mum. I'm sure 'Emo' is just the 21st-century word to describe someone who suffers garden-variety depression. It's really hard for me to claim, now my youngest child has turned thirteen, that my ever-present existential angst is post-natally related.

Emoism, like depression, comes and goes throughout life. It's not whether one suffers from depression that is the issue as much as how you deal with it when it invades your house for a few days, weeks or months.

You don't have to wear a long black trenchcoat, sport charcoal-rimmed eyes, listen to Nirvana, write soul-slashing poetry or cut your arms to qualify as an Emo. Back in the seventies, I was bleeding emotionally just as much while wearing tartan trousers, and singing along to the Bay City Rollers, Abba, Queen and Skyhooks.

'Emo' is not just a dirty word. It's a dark, dank and dismal one. Nor is it a big, fluffy wingless bird that sticks its head in the sand to avoid coping with the realities of life.

It describes a tired, overwrought mother who comes home from earning a pittance working full-time only to discover that her daughter's got yet another body piercing (this time across the back of her neck), the bailiffs have repossessed the plasma TV, and the dog's thrown up on the carpet — again. That's when she sticks her throbbing head into a bucket of vodka-flavoured ice-cream — but not before shouting, 'Triple Bollocks!'

Picture perfect

There's only one job worse than being a paparazzi photographer stalking Hugh Grant in the wee small hours of the morning, and that would have to be being a shopping-centre baby photographer where getting hit in the eye with a can of baked beans is the least of your worries.

If you ever want to see your sweet-tempered, darling baby without warning spit the dummy, just think about taking a photo of them and, like spontaneous combustion, it will happen. Yet, some people actually want to make a living this way.

I'd rather stick a red-hot poker through my brain than spend eight hours a day trying to get the perfect picture of wailing babies with anxious mothers hovering. This while being watched by a crowd of bemused shoppers sniggering at your lame attempts to distract Junior by shaking a teddy bear over your head — and smiling rigidly as sweat drips off the end of your nose. Getting kicked in the telephoto lens by a hot and huffy Hugh Grant would seem like a picnic in the park.

Revenge is sweet, and after many years of me taking endless happy snaps of my children and proudly placing them in the family photo album, my children have turned the tables on this Mumarazzi.

The computer is their weapon of choice to punish me for years of forcing them to smile and say, 'Brie is better' to the blinking red eye. They quietly turn the webcam in my direction and show their scaly schoolfriends just what their slack-jawed mother looks like sprawled out on the couch having an nap.

So I can understand where Hugh Grant is coming from when he hurled a can of Heinz at his endless persecutors.

Tins of baked beans, as well as howls of protest, were thrown at me when I suggested we decorate one wall in the house with family photos. If a picture paints a thousand words, my kids said them all that day, most of them turning the air blue. This was especially so as the youngest child thinks he's adopted, as there are hundreds of pictures of his older brother and sister and about three of him.

And one of those is the obligatory family portrait for which we get dressed up in our good clothes, and stay on our best behaviour, by repressing insulting comments and smiling with clenched teeth, before paying an exorbitant fee to have that magical family moment captured to hang in the lounge room.

Now, there's a picture worth taking.

Road trips — not angry, but all the rage

My daughter and I drove to Mandurah recently, and on that 90-minute trip in the confession-booth atmosphere of her 2000 Lancer with the John Butler Trio playing in the background, I learned more about what she'd done over the past two years than I would have through any amount of stern parental lecturing, evil-eye face-offs, aggressive standover tactics or abusive screaming. The trick, I discovered, is to put on my best therapist face, make it all about her, nod consistently and enthusiastically, and never bang my throbbing head against the closed window, no matter what my bleeding ears were hearing. It was all about lulling her into a false sense of security, putting up and shutting up and giving her enough rope. By the time we got to Meadow Springs, I knew more about her life than any mother would really need or want.

I gained five kilos on that trip. Not from the chocolate, chips and ice-cream we ate, but from all the emotional baggage she unloaded onto me. What she confessed I had suspected for a long time, but now it was out in the open and sitting between us, like a faulty handbrake while going down a steep hill.

Did I really need to know what else had happened that she hadn't told us about at the time the rest of us went camping and left her fifteen-year-old self at home for the long weekend? Mr Corey Worthington, he of the hood, huge yellow sunglasses and infamy, would not have been so bold and brassy. As she said to me, at around the Thomas Road turnoff, 'It was all your fault, Mum; what were you thinking?'

I'm not sure that by this stage I had the capacity for thought. But, somehow, despite my best intentions, my daughter still thinks I'm a good mum, because I listen (or perhaps I'm simply gobsmacked into silence). In a great twist of irony, one of her friends has a mother who's a child psychologist working with troubled youths and he hasn't spoken to her for years.

Despite the shock it can engender, there are worse things than finding out that your kids would prefer to go to the beach than study, have a hankering to work in a hardware store, or want a gap year between school and university in which to flip burgers and party heartily.

From the moment kids can talk, parents should be ordered to listen. It's easy. You can drink wine while they get drunk on their own sense of power. So, I'm taking my oldest son out to lunch. All I need is a restaurant with a smoky, convivial atmosphere.

Show me the money

It's been said that there's no such thing as a free lunch. Or a free life. Unless you're a teenage girl who is working full-time, living in my house, using my hair products and telling all her friends that her mother's ripping her off big time by charging her 30 dollars a week for food and lodging.

Back in the days when Mandurah was an exotic holiday destination, the Mitchell Freeway started and finished at Loftus Street, and a block of land in the northern suburbs cost about the same as a Cold Play concert ticket does today, I was also paying my mother 30 dollars a week board. And, funnily enough, I bitterly resented her money-grubbing fingers in my hard-earned pay packet.

The cost of living has changed considerably, but mother–daughter relationships have not. The fact that my mother used to cook my dinner, clean my bathroom, wash and iron my clothes and lend me her car, as well as working full-time, was completely lost on me. She was the Number One Rip-off Merchant as far as I was concerned, and I couldn't wait for the day that I could afford to move out of home. That would show her!

As my mother before me experienced, trying to educate stay-at-home adult children on the real cost of living is like trying to push a banana through a brick wall. Physically possible, but a lengthy, messy, tedious job.

The mother–daughter Cold War power struggle becomes as hot as a tropical heatwave when the queen bee in the hive demands some money, honey! It's not that I want my daughter to buzz off in the near future, but 30 dollars a week wouldn't pay the rent on a broom closet these days. For the equivalent of ten cans of Red Bull or three packs of cigarettes, she gets, aside from room service, free wireless internet, all food and fridge items, access to my bathroom products, and all the motherly help and advice she could ever want, including a shoulder to cry on.

Cost of raising a child to adulthood — Much more than 30 dollars a week.

Trying to get a regular weekly payment from your freeloading daughter — Your sanity.

Remaining friends with your adult children after they leave home — Priceless.

There are some things that money can't buy, and for everything else, there's the government-funded baby bonus, a means-tested family allowance and the gratification of knowing that one day your children will have children of their own.

The pursuit of perfection

In my perfect world, there would be no weeds, dust, vertical blinds, excess body hair, grey regrowth, acrylic nails, wobbly bits, non-refundable gym memberships, bad school reports, premenstrual tension, smart-mouthed teenagers, body-piercings either below or above the navel, jazz music, Foxtel or typographical errors. Everyone would be happy, well educated, self-actualised and born with the ability to touch-type with 98 per cent accuracy, split infinitives rather than hairs and be able to spell 'diarrhoea' and 'haemorrhage' without the aid of a spellcheck.

In the real, mostly imperfect world, even self-proclaimed perfectionists make mistakes. In fact, most perfectionists try so hard not to make mistakes that, paradoxically, they end up making more. A friend who's a professional writer asked me to 'just take a look' at her up and coming, as yet offline, website, and I found so many minor errors that I became the Typo-Nazi and, with the zest of an evangelistic holy roller, subjected it to a witch-hunt. Instead of seeing hell and brimstone at every turn, I saw grammatical and typographical devils.

I became the June Dally-Watkins, the Queen of the Written Word, and off with the head of anyone who dared commit a typo. But my crown started to get more than a little tight because my head swelled faster than a frustrated teacher can hurl chalk at an illiterate child. The more I perceived my friend's grasp on correct spelling to be tenuous, the more my brain bulged with smugness, to the point that it almost cut off my circulation. This was until the day my son shouted out gleefully that he'd gotten a 'D' for his assignment. Only, it wasn't his assignment, it was mine, and I was expecting an A+ from his English teacher for my efforts. Exasperated because he was getting it all wrong, I'd banished him to the kitchen to do the dishes and completed his homework for him.

Once when I was on a train and saw a man with a government handbook entitled *Litteracy Standards in Australia*, I had to believe it was a play on words, because the alternative was just too terrifying. Another time, I was in a restaurant at which 'chicken tender-lions' was featured as a main course. I couldn't eat anything with a typo in it — I would choke.

Perfectionism, according to psychologists' research, is a disorder rather like anxiety, depression, or being an infuriating, pig-headed, obsessive-compulsive control freak. I've lain awake all night because I made a typo in a casual email to a friend. I've obsessed on the weeds in the front garden to the point where I dream about pulling up and burning the buggers. And I've gone screamingly mad over an almost invisible scratch on my car that mysteriously appeared after a trip to the drag races.

But it's not really about typos, weeds, scratched enamel, or poor grades: it's about self-esteem, self-perception, being 'good enough', agonising over what others think, and simply being human. If no-one ever made a mistake, gossiped or bitched, kicked the letterbox or plotted revenge, life would be wonderfully straightforward, but also perfectly straight and boring, and what on earth would be left to talk about at a dinner party? What a bland old world it would be if Prince Philip never made a public gaffe, if Mischa Barton were never seen in public with orange-peel thighs or Kirstie Alley without age-defying makeup.

And what about the typos that manage to be poignant? My sister told me in an email that she was having a caesarean, and not a virginal birth, as planned; my divorced friend emailed me about a book she wanted to pass on called *The Heartache of Motherhood*, only she called it *The Heartache of Sex*. Some typos, otherwise known as Freudian slips, can reveal a lot about our true selves and feelings.

Perfectionism is cleaning the house before the cleaner arrives, and simply being responsible is tidying up so that the cleaner can do what she gets paid for. Like my grandmother and my mother before me, though, I'm hardwired to scour the bathroom and toilet beforehand. I have one child who *is* perfect, regularly alphabetising my spice rack and asking teachers for special maths homework during the holidays; one child who *thinks* she's perfect, even though her bedroom is a pigsty; and one child who knows that everyone else is the problem. Before I had kids, I thought my life would be perfect once I gave birth.

There are still times when it annoys me that I'm perfect while others, my kids and husband included, aren't. If only they'd try a little bit harder. At this point, I think I need new children, a new husband, or a new mother. Or a new life.

It's liberating, I tell my obsessive-compulsive vegetarian child, to make mistakes and lots of them, even to revel in stupid, stupid ones. Like the time I went out, put the alarm on, closed the door and the alarm went off — I'd forgotten my daughter was still at home. Or the time I forgot to pick her up from child care and received an irate phone call. Or the time, two years in a row, that my husband and I forgot to attend the primary school parents night — we'll burn in hell for that one! Speaking of my husband, he once got to the airport for a business trip 24 hours early. Many years ago, a friend turned up, complete with present and bottle of champagne, for our housewarming party, only she was a week early. We still tease her about it.

Practice makes perfect, but it also intimidates people. When my daughter was eighteen months old, I visited a friend I hadn't seen for many years. Her two-storey mansion was so immaculate that I thought she must have a team of cleaners round the clock, and I thought *I* suffered from perfectionism. This perfectionist was so intimidated that, sadly, the friendship did not endure.

My friend's website isn't perfect, but, just as she is, it's fun and informative, and has taught me how to live with imperfection. Being imperfect, in itself, creates a perfect world for us to live in.

Waiting to email

The first thing I do when I get home from work is kick off my shoes. Then I kick the kids off the computer and into the garden, open a bottle of wine and indulge in my latest addiction — checking my emails to see if I've received any in the time it's taken me to make my 20-minute journey.

Email to me is what breathing is to the next person. Sometimes when I haven't received an email for five minutes, I send one to myself. When I send an email and don't receive an immediate reply, paranoia sets in. Did I say something to offend? Don't they like me anymore?

It doesn't register with me that not everyone sits at a computer all day, ending up with email addiction and a case of what I call 'Internet Arse' — a chronic affliction whereby your bottom starts spreading, like volcanic lava, down the sides of your computer chair.

Six pm comes and goes. My hungry children are pressing their noses against the wrong side of the glass sliding door, but I close the curtains and continue with my inbox.

There's no greater thrill than seeing that sky-blue bar zipping across the screen confirming that, yes, I do have friends. This is until I realise that I'm being asked if I want to increase my penis size, or order some dodgy medication from an even dodgier Mexican hospital, or send my bank account details to the very nice South American Dr Mendez, who kindly wishes to increase my bank balance — and possibly my penis, should I have grown one since his last email — by several million dollars.

I open the curtains and the glass sliding door, put some two-minute noodles on the stove and beckon in the kids.

It's been three minutes since I checked my email and I'm starting to suffer withdrawals.

No email.

Damn it!

I send myself an email to make sure nothing's broken. I do this in the same frenetic manner in which I used to check the phone every five minutes the day after a hot date, waiting for Mr Right to call.

Many years ago, back in the dark ages — say, 1995 — I corresponded with an English friend, and there was a six-week turnaround in letters and replies. And it never used to bother me.

Now, if there's a six-minute turnaround on emails, I get panicky and find myself pounding the refresh button in a manner that should have the men in white coats coming to take me away.

Never email anyone on a Friday or Saturday night. It reinforces to everyone just what a sad life you lead.

Tit for tat

When life gets on your tits, book yourself in for a mammogram. Men, please take note, this is not an Australia Post-designed incentive to get women to send you their bosoms through the mail.

It's also NOT the mammogram represented in the email that's been doing the rounds for years in which part of the preparation involves a woman called Helga, of questionable gender, sticking your boobs between two frozen metal bookends before mashing them together. This picture is so how NOT to prepare for your mammogram.

Anyway, there isn't really any preparation for getting your breasts x-rayed — except for when a lovely lady radiographer heated up her hands to match her warm heart, and gently manipulated my lumpy breasts into the clear plastic sandwich toaster and squashed them flat several times, with abject apologies for doing so. I'm addicted to the pleasure of pain, but it didn't hurt. I told her I was most disappointed, and that if she'd been doing her job right, I'd now be writhing on the floor in the agony of the ecstasy.

So, contrary to popular misconception, there are no sadistic lesbian bitches in military uniform and with tightly pulled steel-coloured hair-buns, itching to flatten your warm, tender breasts into cold submission while taking a cruel and unusual delight in doing so. It was that bloody email that had given me the willies.

There was also the fact that my breasts should not have been under public scrutiny, as puberty was very unkind to me. By the time I was 20, I could tuck my cucumber-like breasts into my socks, and squeezing them into a bra was rather like trying to stuff a kilo of bread dough into a purse.

That was before I discovered private insurance and plastic surgery, and started, at the not-so-tender age of 38, having fantasies about winning wet t-shirt competitions. It was reduction and uplift … or bust! Afterwards, there was the neverending thrill of checking out Pinky and Perky (or, should I say, Perky and Perky) in the bathroom mirror every morning.

(They also became somewhere for my husband to hang his hat every night.) I like to think that, barring a few scars, I now have Lara Bingle's breasts, and I love my twins dearly.

It's my belief, and that of many enlightened women I know, that ultrasounds and mammograms should be freely available to anyone of any age, and that includes men. Breast cancer does not discriminate. According to government policy, one might be too young for a mammogram, but, as we all know, one is never too young for breast cancer.

8

Q. Want a nostalgia trip?

A. TURN OFF THE COMPUTER AND OPEN A WINDOW.

Circular logic

My children appear to have given themselves the gift of circular breathing. But, rather than waste this talent playing the didgeridoo or the bagpipes, my daughter has the ability to simultaneously complain non-stop about her job and scoff a big bag of crisps, without once appearing to draw breath.

Normal breathing, it would appear, is overrated in our house. This is something I can attest to in the wee small hours of the morning, when my husband is at the desperately annoying stage of heavy-breathing just before revving up his snore factor to a level that makes a Boeing 747 engine sound like the low setting on an electric fan.

This is when a set of earplugs comes in handy. Cheaper than marriage counselling, and, unlike cattle prods or pepper spray, perfectly safe and legal. You don't need to shift your husband to the shed to get a good night's sleep; just shove some plastic foam into your ears and all thoughts of smothering him with the spare pillow disappear out the window.

You don't even have to take the earplugs out in the morning, because they work well on trains, planes, buses and automobiles. I love the smell of silence in the early hours, when all I can hear is my own breathing through the dulcet tones of nothingness as I meditate my way through the rush-hour madness.

This is just as well, because my car radio and CD player are on the blink. If I don't meditate, breathe and generally relax my way to work, living with the voices inside my head is like taking a five-year all-expenses-paid vacation in the waiting room of a public hospital emergency department on a Saturday night.

It used to be that you caught the train or bus in the morning with several hundred other like-minded semi-sleep-drugged people. The most noise you would ever hear would be the rustling of the daily newspaper or, on the bus in the halcyon days pre-1975, the flare of a match as someone lit up their early morning cigarette.

Now it's the doof-doof bass thump of someone's iPod, MP3 player, an extraordinarily loud mobile phone conversation about absolutely nothing, or the sound of 55 thumbs frantically text messaging — although why anyone would need to receive a text message at 6 am is beyond me.

Everyone is manically plugged into something and I feel like a bit like a Commodore 64 in a room full of wireless laptop computers. That's when I get out my old-fashioned book and start turning the pages. If an electrical storm wiped out all technology, we'd be cavemen within days. Then we'd be breathing and complaining at the same time.

Perhaps technology is proving that evolution doesn't necessarily always move in a forward direction.

So you think you can dance?

Children are extremely mortified by the many wicked things their parents do, such as existing, buying only unsugared breakfast cereal, or refusing to instal wireless internet and upgrade Foxtel. But, if you really want to scar your children emotionally for life, let them arrive home with their mates to discover that Mum and Dad have not only enrolled in ballroom dancing lessons, but are, in matching lycra thongs, practising the lambada in the lounge room with the curtains wide open and the bay window lit up like the stage of a Broadway musical.

This particular parental behaviour is far more traumatising for any self-respecting teenager than Freud's original primal scene. He believed that the basis of all neurotic behaviour is discovering your parents bonking in bed — or anywhere else, for that matter — and, so it would appear, dirty dancing on the dining-room table has pretty much the same effect. If blazing marital rows or shouting at them in front of their friends isn't enough to send your teenagers into psychotherapy, the thought of Ma and Pa getting hot and heavy doing the slow-rhythm, followed by the evening quick-step, while almost starkers, certainly will.

But the goal of learning how to dance properly wasn't to shock our children's sensibilities any further — that was just a bonus. Having dancing lessons was about spicing up our marriage. Putting a bit of zing and zeitgeist into a relationship that has survived, among other things, 22 years, three teenagers, two midlife crises, several visits from overseas relatives, many unfinished DIY projects, pointless daily arguments with a know-it-all teenage son, and a family trip to Queensland that lasted ten very looong days. Our nuptials needed a boost in the same way a sagging couch either needs reframing, re-covering, revamping or replacing.

But I also needed to overhaul my thoughts on dancing. There were my long-repressed memories of my primary school self learning how to dance to Gary Glitter songs, with grubby little boys who thought that anyone of the opposite sex had 'girl germs'. If that weren't enough, I also had to bury the ghost in my subconscious of my wilting wallflower experiences from that tortuous ritual known as the high school social — a time when the squeaky clean, squeaky voiced Barry Gibb wanted to know how deep was your love.

There's far more to dancing than the hucklebuck, the macarena or the birdie. It's not just about jerking, jiggling, jumping, wiggling and shimmering like a peacock or peahen in heat to 'Nutbush City Limits' once a year at a family wedding; instead, it's an of-the-mind, holistic, all-encompassing experience, rather like condensing a three-week *Sea Princess* cruise into one night. To do it properly, you need The Wardrobe — satiny, body-hugging outfits with exploding, cascading, upflaring skirts, and shoes with 10 cm spikes — and the unwavering belief that if Pauline Hanson can get on *Dancing with the Stars*, so the hell can you.

Getting all dressed up with somewhere to go, without the pesky children, is the ultimate in addictive adult experiences. On Friday nights, the kids might moan and groan and howl in protest, and question us relentlessly about just where do we think we're going dressed like that, but we finally get to shrug dismissively as we are walking through the doorway, and say casually, 'Just out!'

It's always a good thing to turn off your mobile phone at

the dance classes. This isn't because your ringing phone might disturb the atmosphere, but so your kids can't ring up and whinge, and ask when are you coming home, because it's cold, dark and lonely, and that they love you and miss you dearly!

Sorry, what's that? Can't hear you, darlings — bad reception here, the phone's breaking up!

What's in a name

Sticks and stones
may break my bones,
But names will either
give me a life-threatening eating disorder,
or turn me into a serial killer.

Which is what I told my two teenage boys — one who recently got braces and another who recently got glasses.

These hideously expensive facial devices, it would appear, are not for teeth-straightening purposes or to get a clear view of one's immediate surroundings but are, rather, a lame excuse for taking brother-bashing to a completely new level. Verbal sparring over the chops and broccoli has been elevated to an art form by 'Metal Mouth' and 'Four-Eyes'.

When I think of name-calling, I will now always think of Alec Baldwin calling his daughter a 'thoughtless little pig'. If I had a dollar for every time I had mentally called my children thoughtless little pigs, we would have paid off our mortgage years ago.

When I was at school in the seventies, a 'Fat Hairy Mole' was NOT a furry, overweight, ground-burrowing rodent — it was an innocent schoolgirl who was a bit too fond of her chocolate and a bit too young to shave her legs. To this day, I can't watch Discovery Channel documentaries about small animals without the time machine cranking itself all the way back to 1975.

If you have to call someone names, be a little bit witty and creative, and do it to a celebrity who will cry in their limousine all the way to the bank. I've never forgotten un-Cultured Club's Boy George calling Prince a 'dwarf dipped in a bucket of pubic hair', or Clive James's description of Arnie Schwarzenegger as a 'condom full of walnuts', but doing so from the relative safety of another country. (Just as well — I don't think I'd like the Artist Formally Known as Prince chomping on my kneecaps or for the Terminator to have a 'Hasta La Vista, Baby' contract out on me.)

My daughter calls me, among other things, a 'tool' and my friends call me a 'dag'. But just what is a 'dag', anyway? Is it someone:

- who's too un-hip to be square
- who originates from Europe
- who's wickedly cool and endearing or
- something that hangs off a sheep's bum

And while I have no idea what a 'tool' is, aside from those pristine instruments hanging in my husband's shed, my vague understanding is that being called one by your teenage daughter is not exactly a compliment.

So, call me a 'fat, daggy, thoughtless pig of a tool'; just don't call me late for lunch.

Speed cleaning

Speed cleaning is something I used to do back in the late eighties, when amphetamine-based diet pills were all the rage. Those were the days when my self-esteem was based on whether the curtains matched the carpet and complemented the couch and cushions (the very same light-coloured cushions my children now use as a drip-tray for their choc-coated ice-creams).

Apparently, there's a rumour going round that it's humanly possible to keep a house clean in just fifteen minutes a day. It used to take me that long just to gather my strength to scrape the Weet-Bix off the dining-room walls. Now it takes me the best part of quarter of an hour to push my way through the front door, and past all the schoolbags, trombones, rollerblades, over-flowing laundry baskets and lunchboxes that litter the hallway.

This is a household that, at the last census, contained two adults, three semi-adults, two longhaired cats and a fleabag of a dog. My house, like my life, is not spotless. It's full of big spots, small spots and very messy, smelly stains. It's full of ponky areas of unknown origin emanating from the general vicinity of the kitchen. Out damn spot? More like: Out, damn spotty teenagers!

Some people make a living out of other people's messy spots. I went to a micro-fibre cleaning party a few months ago, and drank a bottle of wine and fell asleep, but not before telling the hostess that I thought her product was a pile of overpriced gobshite.

I've found that after a couple of glasses of good wine — bad wine will do in a crisis (and my life is currently one loooong crisis) — on a Friday night, all carpet and furniture spots magically disappear of their own accord. Of course, they do so only to reappear again, in head-splitting fashion, on Saturday morning.

Which is, of course, family housework day. As this became the day I would lose the will to live, I hired a cleaner. At four hours a fortnight — which works out to be roughly seventeen minutes a day — she cleans my house. As long as she squirts lots of bleach-based product around the toilets and showers, the rest is up to her. If the place smells of harsh ammonia-based cleaning products when I come home, I'm happy to pay her more per hour than I make in my own, non-cleaning, job.

She's not so much sanitising and de-spotting my place of residence as restoring tranquillity to my erratic and dysfunctional household.

A passion for fashion

When the Dreamer was twelve, I took him shoe shopping and, after several fruitless hours, he commented that he loves shopping but hates it as well.

'It's called ambivalence,' I said.

'What, you mean the way most kids feel about their parents?' he replied.

But the velcro black sneaker was on the other foot when I mentioned that long-suffering parents also have debilitating bouts of offspring-induced bittersweet emotions.

I'm not ambivalent about some recent fashions, though. I recall a friend lamenting that it was the worst season for fashion she'd ever seen. Just who was it who decided smock tops were going to be worn by un-pregnant women?

You need a decidedly concave stomach to wear one without looking like you're about to drop a pair of 5 kg twins. Not even the human toothpick, Posh Spice, fits into that category. If muffin tops were all the rage not too long ago, the following season's look was definitely 'bun in the oven' wear.

And what's with the capacious handbags these days? If you can fit a fridge under your smock top, you can fit the kitchen sink inside the filing cabinet you're now expected to carry over your right shoulder. I'm carrying more excess baggage than Qantas would allow on board, but, when all's said and done, at least I'm only ever going to the shops or to work, not around the world in 80 different mood swings.

Bring back the days of bell-bottomed jeans and tank tops, when a comb, keys, cigarettes and purse could fit into your back pocket, leaving your bare arms free and swinging, and loose enough to discipline the kids with. If you were out enjoying yourself in the good old days, you only ever rang anyone, from a public phone box when it was a life-or-death situation, not because you felt the overwhelming need to have a family member check your email every five minutes.

When you are closer to menopause than you are to puberty, life becomes more about minimisation and less about bleaching your toilet on a daily basis and other endless, unappreciated housework, stressing over emotionally messy family situations or wearing tragically uncomfortable fashion garments and carrying gigantic hold-all accessories with the potential to dislocate your right shoulder and topple you off your 10 cm spikes.

Back to basics, I say. If the shoe fits, don't only wear it, but buy another 24 pairs — each in a different shade and colour.

Mobile phony

Separation anxiety is a normal stage of human development. An example of it is when a two year old can't bear to let Mummy out of their sight. Adult separation anxiety occurs when we can't bear to let our mobile phone out of our sight.

I left my mobile at home on the day my last child finally went to school. I still think the reason our house got robbed was that I was high-fiving everyone I came in contact with the day all three kids attended the same school at the same time. My phone was stolen and I suffered more separation anxiety due to that than I did due to leaving my youngest at kindergarten.

Urban legend has it that mobile phones were invented so that if your car broke down, you could call the RAC and not risk getting chopped up by an axe murderer. I don't think it was so that your teenage children could text each other to 'pass tmto srs b4 I hit u' at the dinner table.

Nor was it invented so that we could text random thoughts to passing strangers. Sending random randy thoughts to your spouse, though, has been known to spice up a flagging sex life. Just ask an aging would-be Lothario spin bowler or my husband when he's on a business trip. Once, just as dawn broke, I got a horny text message. We sex-texted for a while, till I sent 'Is that you, Shane' and got the reply 'Oh my God it's the wife!'

This piece of 20th century technology is less about wireless communication than it is about being able to command a captive audience on the train to work. It's a means of letting everyone know how wonderful your life is, how good your holiday in Fiji was or how indispensable you think you are to your workplace. If all the world's a stage and we are merely players, public transport is where the average person delivers an Oscar-winning performance.

The volume of the speaker seems always to be in direct relation to the quietness of the train. If the person two seats behind can hear you, you're too loud. When the people in the train behind can hear you, it's time to get a job as a police siren.

Nobody cares as much about your life as you do and I had always known that the rest of the world was not as fascinated by my mobile phone calls as I was. But then I got the phone call from work while on the train and biology took over and the adrenaline coursed. As well as the fight or flight response, there now exists the phone response, by which my chest puffed up and my voice got deeper and louder as I realised how important I actually was.

The sad part was that I was fully aware of what was happening and yet was unable to stop myself. It was easier to stop my heart from beating than it was to decrease my volume, and the more trouble I had hearing the person at the other end, the louder I got. Even though I was cringing inwardly, I just couldn't shut up.

It was easier to just get off at the next station whether it was my stop or not.

Single mum with triple trouble

If my unruly and outspoken children spoke to their friends the way they speak to each other and to their parents, they would soon have none left. Having spent much of my early years an only child raised on the parent-friendly 'Famous Five' books, I now find my brain twisting into hideous spasms every time I see my children open their mouths to shout some more atrocious abuse at each other.

Julian, Dick, George and Anne would rather have stoically accepted a well-deserved spanking than sully their stiff upper lips giving Uncle Quentin or Aunt Fanny some sarky backchat. Not so with my children. Sarkyness isn't in short supply in our household, spankings are something that happens to a monkey, and the feral factor was upped considerably when their father flew interstate for two weeks, leaving me a very single mother celebrating a milestone birthday by taking her kids out for dinner.

Arriving at the local Chinese restaurant, Environmentally Conscious, Vegetarian Son, secretly dubbed 'Save the Snails', would not sit down till he found out whether the squeaky black chairs were made of vinyl or of blood-on-their-hands leather. All this while my other, environmentally un-conscious, non-vegetarian 'Stomp the Snails' children drooled over the various deceased-animal dishes on the menu. (This was the place I discovered that, contrary to popular opinion, pink prawn crackers do not contain anything even vaguely resembling a dead crustacean.)

Trying to avoid controversial topics, I made an innocent remark about what lovely weather we'd been having, which brought on a heated argument about the causes and consequences of global warming and the El Niño effect. Somehow, greenhouse gases had become all my fault, due to my love of cigarettes, wood-burning fires and of squirting mozzies with Mortein.

So, it was Pick on Mum Time. When my three kids get together and are in a silly mood, peer pressure and pack mentality rule, and, like The Children of the Damned, they tune into their extraordinary telepathic powers and turn against The Other.

At this crucial point, law and order can only be restored with the promise of fried ice-cream, and the threat of sending their absent father mobile-phone video of their bad behaviour that includes food fights in a public place. Twenty-first century technology allows 'Just wait till your father gets home' to take on a whole new meaning.

This is something that would have had Enid Blyton tut-tutting in her grave.

Tell me no secrets

There's no point having a secret unless you can tell it to someone.

Like money, and children with pyromaniac propensities, classified and confidential information can burn a hole, laser-like, through the shallow recesses of my brain. Like a subdural haematoma, the pressure can only be relieved when the contents are spilled. But loose lips sink ships and, in the past, my beak has leaked enough information to sink the *Titanic*.

A secret by any other name is still a secret if you only tell one person. This is the rule of secrets. The other is knowing who to tell and when. If you don't want your mother to know that you once wagged first-year high school in order to drool over Steve McQueen and Paul Newman in *The Towering Inferno*, don't say a word to anyone. Ever.

My head sways and burns, throbs and bulges, if someone lays bare their deepest confidence and I know I cannot reveal it. But no amount of pain, even if a group of American soldiers have me lain out on the stretch rack, will make me reveal the secrets of a Girls' Night In.

That's because girls' nights in are all about sharing secrets, as opposed to accidentally spilling one's guts in an inappropriate fashion (a different matter entirely). Secrets are best shared on a Saturday night over a bottle, or six, of wine, the idea being that the very nature of the enterprise is to swap secrets of equal magnitude.

So, not so long ago, when the children were safely tucked up in bed, a friend and I settled down in our ugg boots and tracky dacks to a chicken tikka, took the strawberry champagne off ice, and got down to the pressing matter of finding out exactly where each other's emotional bodies were buried.

Along with character assassinations of friends, relatives and co-workers, nothing bonds two females tighter than two layers of lipstick than does hard gossip and intuitive innuendo. These are sometimes based mainly on a charged glass of alcohol and a vivid imagination.

But that's OK, because of 'the *Seinfeld* Factor': that is, that all secrets, without exception, must on nights like these be cared and shared and then locked in the vault forever. A cared-and-shared mutual exposure takes the pressure off the brain.

In fact, part of the pleasure is in knowing that your sordid little secrets are as safe as hers are. Especially if there is video evidence on your mobile phone.

Hmm, I might do a ring-around. I feel another girls' night in coming on.

What employers want

What do employers want? What are they looking for in an employee who is possibly going to be in their face for the next 20 or 30 years?

Apparently, the key buzzword is 'versatility', along with having a 'can-do' attitude. This is what sorts out the Paris Hiltons from the Condoleeza Rices. (I do have reason to believe that Paris is extremely versatile — just in a completely different way from what most employers want.)

So, after a few weeks of looking for a full-time job, I managed to convince an employer that I have 'can-do' versatility — in the good way, of course — during the hours of nine to five. However, I failed to mention that for the rest of the time, I'm a control freak with obsessive-compulsive tendencies.

And I'm trying obsessively and compulsively to repress the dark memories of other interviews, including the one for a job that would have required me to wear black tights and an above-the-knee checked uniform that bore an alarming resemblance to the one I was forced to wear as a Catholic schoolgirl. There's not a big enough pay packet in the world to induce me to catch the early morning train looking like a green-and-white checkered beach ball.

Almost as alarming as that particular image is the trend of employers asking pseudo-psychological questions that bear about as much relevance to the job applied for as Nicole Kidman does to real-life parenting.

One employer asked me what the most important issue in my life was and why. What sort of issue? A financial one? Achieving world peace? Or the fact that my cat died three years ago and I'm still not over it?

Then he asked. Can I Excel?

I can Excel at anything you want me to, I say.

'Can you do Windows?'

'I have a can-do attitude towards Windows. I positively Excel at Window shopping till I'm dropping.'

'Are you willing to be flexible?'

'I'm trying my hardest but just can't seem to touch my toes. However, placing my foot in my mouth doesn't seem to require a great degree of difficulty.'

'What about spreadsheets?'

'What on earth has bedroom linen got to do with the price of eggs, you silly man?'

While we're on the subject of fatuous thinking, my Catholic-church-going father said that if he were an employer and had to choose between this degree and that qualification, he would choose the girl with the biggest breasts. My husband nodded his head in total agreement.

I hear there are still plenty of jobs going begging in the local papers. However, fat, flat-chested, fuming, 40-something applicants need not apply.

Zen and the art of closet clutter

After years of ranting and raving at our children to clean up their bedrooms, they finally cottoned on to the fact that their parents' bedroom and walk-in robe, which resembled the morning after a wild teenage party, was, in fact, far worse than theirs.

Most people lock up their house to keep the devil out. But there are more demons behind the bulging door of my dark closet than there are out on the shadowy streets at night.

So, armed with my Zen minimalist mindset, breathing in and out slowly to the mantra that 'Less is more', I ventured forth into the closet. First to hit the highway was ANYTHING with shoulder pads that made me look like Priscilla, Queen of the Desert.

This included the black pinstriped power suit I wore with black net stockings and high-heeled shoes to a daggy call centre I used to work at. This was the sort of place where beer-brand t-shirts and lycra leggings prevailed, and wearing purple polyester slacks was considered dressing up. I felt about as comfortable as Princess Anne at a bash in *Kath and Kim*.

There are some things at the back of one's wardrobe that should never be displayed. Such as a complete collection of Gary Glitter records (I can't play them now without feeling troubled and nauseous); a pack of playing cards displaying 52 explicitly naked men; a box of motivational weight-loss tapes; several empty chocolate boxes; my first and last attempt at a Mills & Boon manuscript; two positive pregnancy test sticks; and a box of gruesome-looking baby teeth.

Sitting high on a shelf, beneath the broken record player, was the crumpled box containing my wedding dress, which made its one and only public appearance back in the mid-eighties. I wanted to ditch it, but my husband and sons didn't, in case our daughter wanted to get married in it.

Seeing as there are times that she can't bear to sit on the same couch as me, the prospect of my daughter wearing my wedding dress on her special day is about as remote as Paul McCartney and Heather Mills renewing their wedding vows in a haze of blissful forgiveness.

Now that the wardrobe is clean and tidy, it's time to clear the rest of the house of all useless and annoying clutter. That's when the cats, dog and children get rather anxious, and even my husband starts to look at me cautiously.

9

Q. What do flatulence, bloodsucking creatures and teenagers have in common?

A. THEY'RE REALLY AWFUL THINGS THAT NEED TO BE REPRESSED IMMEDIATELY.

Going nuts with nits and lice

If you have lots of animals and children in your house, chances are that you have fleas and lice in abundance as well.

These little creatures, rather like your irritating offspring, live there rent-free, embarrass you enormously with their presence, and make you irritable and itchy to the point that you just wish they'd go and live somewhere else.

No-one ever admits to fleas and lice squatting in their home: it's a bit like having an STD, or admitting you once voted for Pauline Hanson. You never, ever talk about it at the hairdresser's and it simply doesn't come up during dinner-party conversations. It's more like a deathbed confession.

But I've been scratching my head ferociously over this issue for a long time now. This was especially so at work the other day, when I felt something crawl from one side of my scalp to the other, and knew that I had to suppress that scream for at least another eight hours till I could get home and throttle the kids.

According to urban legend, lice only like beautiful, clean, shiny hair. This theoretically should rule out the heads of my two boys, because they seem to think sulphuric acid, not shampoo, pours out of those expensive salon bottles. They wash their hair once a month whether they need to or not, and that's only when I threaten to join them naked in the shower and do it for them. It's one of life's enduring mysteries that boys can go through an entire bottle of shampoo in one hit only to have their hair still smell like hair at the end of it.

If all the tiny hair- and fur-dwelling creatures in our house paid board, we could retire to Tahiti next week. We have fruit flies in the fruit bowl, even when there's no fruit in it; we open the pantry and more moths fly out than when a government opens its wallet before an election.

We leave the Hoover on standby for all the big, hairy spiders that crawl out through the paint in the walls, and, despite regular costly baths, the cats and dog scratch out enough fleas to fill up a pit. That's when it's high time to drop a few insect bombs.

There's nothing quite like a huge mushroom cloud of toxic, cancer-inducing chemicals to make the house feel wonderfully clean and safe for human habitation again.

Thirteen

The only time you'll have all the answers to all life's questions, and then some, is when you hit the age of thirteen, and could fly yourself to the moon and back fuelled solely by your own egocentric self.

My older boy and I went out for a mother–son pre-shopping dinner at a local restaurant. When a pretty young waitress, who went to the same school as him, apologised for leaning over while placing cutlery in front of him, he uttered drolly, 'I could SO get you fired for that!'

Pretty, young schoolfriend waitress and I looked at him, looked at each other and burst out laughing. Luckily, he had the good grace to look both sheepish and charmingly foppish, in a Hugh Grant way.

But then, on the basis of two weekends' work in another local restaurant, he set about criticising every aspect of the décor, menu, and the rest of the hardworking staff who produced our lovely meal. This from the boy who doesn't know where our dishwasher is, let alone how to put a plate in it, while also being under the delusion of adequacy that the restaurant he worked in would collapse unless he turned up once a week for his job as a kitchen hand.

However, it's a misconception I am loath to correct because we all need to feel omnipotent at some stage in our short, sad lives. This, unfortunately, tends to get beaten out of us when we get a real job in the real world, and end up with a really big mortgage and some really irritating children to raise for the next 20 years or more. That's when you realise that you're not even sure what the original burning question was, let alone the snappy existential answer.

After dinner, my son and I went shopping for new clothes for his upcoming music trip to England. He didn't quite get the idea that there was no possible way that his teenage self was going to represent School and Country wearing a windcheater extolling the virtues of popular beers and of Jim Beam whisky.

Still, his 'I'm King of the World' kitchen-hand experiences will come in handy for his trip, as, in a moment of sheer genius, I mentioned to his host family that one of his biggest likes is washing dishes.

Ah! Thirteen! Unlucky for some. But for others, a chance to travel to another country while the rest of us languish at home.

John and Janette sitting in a tree

If a bad-taste moment was discovering that former prime minister John Howard and his wife, Janette, still hold hands in public after 30 years of marriage, a worse taste moment was discovering that another former prime minister's wife finds public displays of love disgusting.

Marriage is the closest thing to a life sentence most of us will ever endure, so we may as well make the best of it. Now that the kids are getting older, things are finally getting better in our household. My husband and I aren't just holding hands.

One morning, he and I got out of bed, went into the kitchen, gave each other a warm, passionate hug, and commented that it was no wonder we were so tired. My older son, who had been quietly minding his own business and eating corn flakes, suddenly started screaming and banging his traumatised head against the wall.

His actions were much like what the former prime minister's wife must have felt like doing when the story broke. Politicians, especially John Howard, have never featured in my wildest sexual fantasies, although Al Gore is starting to look mighty fine these days. And, while I don't want to hold John Howard's hand, or anything else for that matter, I do, like a lot of women, have a wild urge to give his eyebrows a good plucking.

When spring has sprung, love is in the air. Everywhere. Not just at Kirribilli House, but in my pantry, where the weevils do the wild thing in the Weet-Bix. And in my neighbour's pool, where frogs frolic with reckless abandon at night.

So, it came as no surprise when, at that time of year, sex education started rearing its not-so-ugly head at our younger son's primary school.

After an informative lesson in 'Doing What They Do on the Discovery Channel', the class was asked to write down what qualities one should look for in a good, caring relationship. My son wrote, 'Commitment, Respect and Personal Hygiene'. The boy next to him wrote, 'Big Boobs and a Big Arse'. This outlook is just one of the subtle differences between John Howard and, let's say, Bill Clinton.

And there's a vat of difference between sour grapes and a nice mellow glass of wine. Thirty years, in fact. Methinks the former 'first lady' doth protest too much.

Smutty, smuttier, smuttiest

Friends of ours have six children living under their roof, and they have my complete admiration — as well as my therapist's phone number.

It must mean that twice as much swearing goes on in their household as it does in mine. With my three kids spitting and hissing expletives at each other, the air frequently turns varying shades of bloody-minded blue.

'So, where the bloody hell are you?' is less an unsuccessful tourism campaign slogan than it is what every Saturday night I scream down the mobile phone at my curfew-breaking Wild Child, who feels that she can 'bloody well do what she bloody well pleases'. Only it's not actually the word 'bloody' that she uses.

I fine her a dollar every time she swears and, so far, she owes me the equivalent of Australia's national credit card debt. Not that I've ever really believed that my ineffectual bleatings of 'Stop bloody swearing' are likely to have any effect on her or her brothers. This is in contrast to the time that, as a teenager in the mid-seventies, I told my father to 'Get knotted' and copped a bloody good hiding for my efforts.

The Queen's English is to my children what subtlety is to mother-in-law jokes. When my kids were younger, smutter wouldn't melt in their mouths, so I dragged them off to the bathroom to wash the not-so-royal words out of their mouth with soap. But I can't do that anymore — they are much bigger than I am.

So, now I try to tell them that anyone can swear and that it takes a stronger, better person to think of a replacement adjective, but they tell me that I don't know what the bloody hell I'm talking about. Still, if it was thought to be OK to swear in a campaign promoting Australia overseas, what hope do we parents have?

It's not that I'm against foul language per se. I've been known to use the f-word on many occasions, especially while giving birth. I can swear as good as the next mother, just as long as my children are in earshot.

I know this smacks of hypocrisy, of 'do as I say — not as I do!', but we mothers seem to have an infinite capacity for displaying inconsistent behaviour. It's the only way we can bloody well survive the world of manky teenage behaviour.

Royal showoffs

The Perth Royal Show, like school fees, council rates and Christmas, comes once a year and costs just as much as they do. So, before the last one, I emptied out the nearest ATM, made an appointment with a chiropractor for the following day, and my youngest child and I hit Sideshow Alley.

My son is mature for his age and I'm immature for mine, so we met in the middle. Again, I got in touch with my inner bad boy, which, for this middle-aged mother, is never far away. It was only between the bumper cars and the Python Loop that I realised I wasn't immortal or thirteen (which is the same thing when you're actually that age) after all, and that I'd left the Nurofen Plus at home.

But even bumper cars are tame and lame compared with the towering Mega Drop. I was lured with knee-bent promises by my son that he would finish his paper round on time if I'd join him in getting sucked into the clouds only to be dropped 45 metres back to earth in 1.8 seconds at 5.5 g-forces.

This would be an average day's work for James Bond or for a St George's Terrace window cleaner. While I'm not a British secret agent and nor do I do dirty windows, I really wanted him to finish (or, at least, start) his paper delivery (sometimes sane people do crazy things just so that the rest of their suburb can read the local news).

The insanity isn't in choosing to do the death drop itself, it's in electing to endure the 60-second wait up in the sky before you drop. It was a sickening mixture of dread and anticipation, which somehow reminded me of childhood, and my mother constantly telling me, 'Wait till your father gets home!' It was an emotion so compelling that my son and I joined the line to experience it again and again.

Afterwards, with my feet planted firmly on the ground, I did what all self-respecting 40-something housewives should do, and wandered slowly round the agricultural halls to check out the dried-flower arrangements, the jams and the decorative wedding cakes.

It's easier to pull a bloodhound past a sausage factory than it is to drag an adrenaline-charged adolescent boy away from the fire and brimstone of Sideshow Alley. So, I left him spinning on a gas-lift office chair by the exhibit door while I admired the fruit scones.

My son and I then ate our way round the rest of the show, avoiding healthy Yellow Brick Road food as much as possible, and watched the horse show and the fireworks.

Despite feeling decidedly seedy, we both fell asleep on the train journey home, but not before my son confided to me that we had had way too much fun for a mother and son.

Things your mother never told you

My mother, who was a product of a 1950s upbringing, never told me what to expect from life. But my children, products of the new millennium, constantly update me on what they've learned, what they expect and how they expect it, and who they expect it from — me, of course.

Currently the hottest item on the teenage dinner-table menu isn't reheated chicken and chips but the issue of the double standards that men, and society generally, impose on women. Why girls are classified either as sluts or virgins, and why boys can pass wind and shout congratulations to each other on doing so, while girls who do it are mortified for life.

My teenage daughter and her friends ask why girls have to sit elegantly cross-legged, whether wearing skirts or jeans, while boys seem evolutionarily compelled to sit with their legs so far apart it looks like they're suffering from hip dysplasia.

Why CAN boys order triple cheeseburgers, a large chips and a thickshake without batting an eyelid, while girls order a small salad and Diet Coke and are in an agony of guilt over the entire 33 kilojoules consumed?

Why can some boys loll comfortably around the house clad only in a pair of boxer shorts while some girls feel uptight and self-conscious sitting straight-backed in a turtle-neck jumper, jeans and ugg boots?

As much as I like to regard myself as a thinking person, I'm still a product of my strict Catholic upbringing, in which bad posture and bodily functions that took place from the neck down were actively discouraged. So, I expect my daughter to sit with her legs together and her hands crossed in her lap, with her bottom clenched to suppress painfully her overwhelming need to release bodily wind.

Reality is different, though, and I'm discovering that the gap between double standards is closing quicker than the butt cheeks of a Yoga instructor. While I'm STILL having therapy about once having accidentally passed wind in a very public place, in October 1979, my daughter passes wind like a man, loudly and exuberantly.

In fact, all my kids chase each other round the house and sit on each other expressly for the purpose of passing wind.

They've even been known to record the sound of it on their mobile phones and use it as a ring tone.

This could be why MY mother, who would rather delicately implode and die than issue an embarrassing sound from her nether regions, somehow knows instinctively only ever to ring us on our home phone number.

Crime and punishment

Setting boundaries has lately become a BIG issue in our household. Whenever I try to establish a framework for crime and punishment, my kids gang up on me and yell in unison, 'Empty threat! Empty threat!'

So, recently I stuck to my guns regarding disciplinary action. The Dreamer asked if he could instal a new program on our computer and, after I answered with an emphatic and resounding 'No!', he went and did it anyway, as 'no' apparently means 'yes' in our household.

He then crashed and burned the computer. (Thank goodness he isn't old enough to borrow, crash and burn the family car; that's his job in a few years.)

Much to his dismay, my son got sent to bed without a nourishing evening meal, and was told that the 200 dollars he'd saved through amateur installation would now be spent on computer repairs. The words 'empty threat' disappeared quicker than sugary breakfast cereal during school holidays — along with his money and his dreams of owning a PlayStation 2.

This all reminds me of the story of when I was five years old and whinged and whined for the packet of peanuts Dad had bought for after dinner. In the end, he threw them out the car window. I don't actually remember this, but whenever the subject of boundaries rears its ugly head, Dad, with devilish delight, tells that tale.

When my daughter was eight years old and whinged and whined for the packet of jelly beans I had bought for her to have after dinner, I followed Dad's example and threw them down the toilet. I was then flushed with guilt when the multi-coloured, gelatinous mass glued itself to the bottom of the loo basin.

But setting hard and fast rules and the 'This is going to hurt me more than it hurts you' approach isn't always the one I take. I sometimes lose The Battle for Boundaries when, for a peaceful life, I'd rather just give in.

Feeding the cats and dog twice a day, for weekly pocket money, is apparently less about emptying a tin of sloppy meat into a plastic bowl than it is an exercise in which boy can triumph in loudly debating the merits of getting his brother to do it instead. I end up feeding the starving animals while brotherly fisticuffs go on in the background.

So, all the cash I save by not giving them their pocket money can go towards a well-deserved holiday for my husband and me — one that will definitely be without the children.

Waves of guilt

I tend to do a lot of surfing these days. This is not at the beach, as we are not a beach family. Rather, it was lucky that I was wearing my life jacket while recently surfing the internet, because waves of guilt suddenly came crashing over the computer and dumped me into the deep sea of despair.

I'd found a report that said that, according to a Perth-based medical research team, 'babies who are breast-fed for less than six months are likely to develop mental health problems in childhood'.

This is just what we already post-natally-depressed, guilt-and-shame-ridden mothers need. More enlightened, groundbreaking research proving what Dr Spock knew all along — it's not your fault you're neurotic or psychopathic, it's your mother's.

Thanks to this medical research team, I now know why I'm a mentally deficient basket case. I was bottle-fed. There's hope for my breast-fed-for-nine-months daughter, but I've changed the names of my two bottle-fed sons to Dumb and Dumber.

Does such research also mean that all disposable-nappy-wearing toddlers are predestined to become environmentally careless deviants when they grow up? Will they have inherent, mother-induced, desires to become politicians or chief executive officers of multinational corporations? Or will they end up as North Korean leaders with their fingers poised over the red button? (I've often wondered whether Darth Vader was breast- or bottle-fed.)

If you want to know what breast-feeding can sometimes feel like, stick your nipples — or, if you're a man, any other sensitive part of your body — into the hose of the vacuum cleaner, and set it to maximum turbo velocity and let it suck for at least an hour. Then repeat every four hours for the next six months, and we'll see who ends up insane.

Sixteen years down the track, I still have self-condemning thoughts, dreams and fantasies in which I'm still desperately expressing breast milk into my kids' corn flakes in an effort to stave off future mental illness.

There are lies, damn lies, and then there is groundbreaking medical research. But all brain-impaired bottle-fed babies, including myself, can take heart at the thought that while mother's milk might have turned sour initially, there is in later years, when all else fails, plenty of healthy goodness in long-term psychotherapy.

Gift wrapped

Christmas is the time of year when generalised anxiety and suppressed memories keep popping up like the gift that keeps on giving. I know this, because every year I lose the will to live at the thought of having to find and buy 200 presents for everyone I've ever met in the past three decades. Never confuse 'Christmas shopping' with 'retail therapy'.

When finally you can't put the deed off any longer, hype yourself up with several double shots of espresso. Also leave your rational brain behind, right next to the large vodka and tonic you've prepared for when you come home (and that loving feeling of Christmas spirit should be drunk as quickly as possible for maximum effect).

Retail rage is the new road rage, which is why I wear my shopping shield. This is an invisible, impenetrable cone of silence that comes in handy when barging through the swarms of shoppers like a warrior entering the battle fray.

Clutching my junk mail catalogues, I make my way towards Electrical Goods to buy a DVD player for the car. Now, when

I was young, most cars didn't have a radio, let alone a home-theatre system with wide screen and surround sound. In order to see moving pictures, you looked out the window, not at the back of the seat in front of you. Mum used to sing to us and 'I Spy' was about as technical as travel entertainment got.

Then, head to Toys, and for the unsuspecting girls there's, of course, half-price Bikini Beach Barbie, which comes with a guaranteed eating disorder. If your daughter's not bingeing and purging within six months, you get your money back, no questions asked.

And the fun doesn't end there, because you now have to spend the rest of your life at the checkout. But, with my shopper shield intact, I indulge in some self-guided meditation while everyone around me is huffing and puffing themselves into a spectacular Michael-Richards-style meltdown. I stand still, and visualise myself under a gentle waterfall in a rainforest, or finding the perfect palm tree on a sun-drenched sandy beach. This then whips up a lusty image of Daniel Craig emerging from the sea glistening and wet, and wearing only a pair of powder-blue budgie smugglers.

And I come home full of peace and goodwill — feeling slightly shaken, but not in the least stirred.

10

Q. Why do I kiss my son while twisting his earlobes?

A. JUST ONE OF THE MANY WAYS TO EXPRESS MOTHER LOVE.

Mothers and sons

When I phone home from work to find out if my boys have arrived there safely from school, and am given a resounding reassurance that the house is NOT on fire, I can't tell just who has answered the phone. They both sound exactly the same to me.

That is, till recently, when my older boy's voice started to break. But that's not all. He now has a serious girlfriend and my heart is also in danger of cracking.

The most special relationship in the world is that between a mother and son. Especially a son who's physically and emotionally changing right before her eyes, when clearly she would prefer him to stay in nappies and OshKosh dungarees.

Instead, he wears braces on his teeth and, thanks to adolescent hormones, his formerly straight hair now sports a Greg-Brady-style perm (his nickname at high school is 'Pubes'). This is all on top of him speaking in a voice that promises to be deeper than a conversation at a convention on Freudism.

I love my older boy truly, madly, deeply, as only a mother can. So, it was traumatic when on a family trip to New Norcia that included his new girlfriend, I turned round and found him holding hands with her, and gazing soulfully into her eyes in exactly the same way he used to look into mine when I read him a Peter Rabbit story.

It bordered on the ridiculous one night that I dropped his girlfriend off. I had to listen to them say a goodbye that entailed all possible 'kissy, kissy, smoochy, lip-smacky, smacky' sounds from the back of the car, as they pashed on without a care in the world. And this was only so that Romeo and Juliet could be prised apart long enough to get home and spend another eight hours on the phone, before dreaming about each other. While I was trying hard not to listen, I found my jaw clenching tightly, and my scalp heating and itching ferociously.

It's not that his girlfriend isn't nice. This isn't about her. This is about me and Mother Love, the type of combination that can, at best, produce a mummy's boy and, at worst, produce a Norman Bates or Seymour Skinner.

I'm having to learn the hard way that sometimes the best love a mother can show her adolescent son is to let go and let someone else take care of her precious bundle of joy.

The lawnmower man

There's never a time in our house when the walls are not shaking violently with the intrusive roar and thunder of hot-headed and opinionated people who resemble Derryn Hinch banging on about a controversial issue. Some members of my family have been known to scream dogmatic views even in their sleep and it's not unheard of for someone else to scream back an opposing view.

So, a short time ago when I was relaxing in the cool, dignified atmosphere of my therapist's office and someone next door fired up a lawnmower, I suffered a panic attack and threw myself against the back wall. My therapist told me, Buddha-like, that I should learn to love the voice of the lawnmower, and embrace it in a holistic, mindful fashion rather as I should Rugs a million adverts, self-administered cotton-wool-bud eardrum stabbings, and other brain-invaders including my nerve-shattering family. I looked at her sideways and backed out the door.

I think she might have been talking about my older son. He has fitted out his scooter with a petrol-driven whipper-snipper motor, and spends so much time revving up the engine with his right hand that he's now suffering from repetitive strain injury. I need to learn to love the sound of, not a lawn mower, but a whipper snipper in the morning. But it's so loud, there are people in our street who think we're hiding a Harrier jump-jet in our garage.

Sometimes when you want to throttle your kids, the best thing to do is to get down and dirty with them and learn how to push a throttle yourself. Like the noise that so often assaults your brain, get inside your children's heads and find out what it is about fossil-fuelled pastimes that they enjoy so much.

While the smell of burning rubber is to me what the smell of Chanel No 5 is to my older son — that is, something to be studiously avoided at all costs — I not only went go-karting but I did it without some therapeutic shopping for perfume, just so that I could spend some time with him.

It's easier to indulge in activities that are enjoyable — such as reading in the sun with a glass of wine, with your personal speedometer accelerating all the way up to zero — than it is to have my bum squashed into thin moulded plastic that skims the bitumen at a bone-jarring 70 kilometres per hour. But I was determined that my son, who thinks I get dizzy watching goldfish swim around a bowl, would acknowledge I had some street cred.

It was three laps before I could take my foot off the brake; another three before I discovered the accelerator; and another three before the need for speed suddenly took over, and I revved up and threw myself into the curves, skidding across the gravel and becoming one with my machine.

Now I know why speed, the non-pharmaceutical variety, is highly addictive. While the Speed-of-Mum doesn't quite have the g-force ripples of the Speed-of-Son, afterwards we both had an overwhelming impulse to rent *The Fast and the Furious*. I learned later, though, that it had been the toxic petrol fumes that made me do it.

I now love the sound of lawnmower in the morning. Just as long as it's my son who's behind it, cutting and collecting the grass, and putting it out with the rubbish.

Dream on

I have a dream. A recurring one, which I started having around about the time my beautiful, compliant children turned into argumentative, snotty, grotty, spotty Teenage Mutant Whingeing Turds.

In my dream, I'm racing around Fremantle trying to rent a one-bedroom flat. I go to one and, upon entering, the door won't lock behind me, the walls fall apart, and all these horrible, scungy, demanding, disturbingly familiar people who vaguely resemble my family surround me, invading my privacy, touching me, and causing my skin to break out in angry red hives and itch ferociously. I wake up in a cold sweat, scratching myself all over.

Getting to pay your children a nominal amount of board, as I understand it, is more about educating your children that there's no such thing as a free lunch, breakfast or dinner. (Even fresh air will cost you, if you breathe it in my house.) What my daughter pays me doesn't even cover my Panadol bill at the local chemist, or make a dent in the cost of her overdue DVD rental fines. Buying your own makeup, shampoo, clothes and jewellery does not count as a contribution to household expenses, I tell her repeatedly, but it falls on deaf, multi-pierced ears.

Her view is that I'm a sadist cracking the whip for her to pick up smelly clothes off a dirty bedroom floor and put them in the washing machine, and then have the temerity to charge her.

A friend of mine works full-time and studies part-time. After one week of home-schooling her primary-aged child, she had the strong urge, backed up by vivid dreams, to flee to Lahore and join the Mujahadeen instead.

I would love to hitch a ride with her but, with what my daughter pays me, I'd be lucky to make it to the end of the street.

I hate you, don't leave me

There's a pull in all of us that's stronger than the gravitational force that keeps the moon spinning around the earth and the earth revolving around the sun. Called 'attachment process', it's the biological super glue that bonds families together, the psychic equivalent of maximum-strength hairspray that keeps your locks attached in place even during a tornado — a structural device without which life as we know it would become, well, detached.

But attachment also has an evil twin. This is the way that, while you can't live without your family, you sometimes wish they'd rent the house next door, or migrate to the lower zones of Antarctica and be in suspended animation for the rest of your life.

George Lucas knew all about attachment process and its counterpart. The force in the *Star Wars* movies is based on the lighter and darker motives that propel human relationships either forwards, towards enlightenment, or backwards, towards regression and disintegration. Scratch the surface of any loving mother or father, and there's a potential Darth Vader lurking beneath.

A long, long time ago, in a research laboratory far, far away, attachment theorist and psychologist John Bowlby conducted separation and reunion experiments, called 'The Strange Situation', with mothers and babies. They were done in order to study the mystical, magnetic duct tape that binds the genetic universe together.

Under laboratory conditions, a mother and her baby would be placed in a room that had two-way mirrors. A stranger would enter and the mother would leave for a short period of time. When the mother returned, her baby's reaction to her absence and to the presence of the stranger was recorded.

Approximately 60 per cent of the babies cried in a distressed fashion but settled quickly and easily when their mothers returned. This was the normal response, called secure attachment. About 20 per cent of the babies showed remarkably little outward anxiety, and when their mothers returned, they didn't seem that interested in reconnecting. This became known as avoidant attachment style. The other 20 per cent of babies became anxious and distressed upon separation, and became angry as well as jubilant when reunited with the their mothers, and so both approached and avoided contact. This contradictory response became known as anxious attachment style. Bowlby's theory was that the attachment style initiated in childhood continues in an unconscious fashion for the rest of our lives.

Many years ago, when my family were camping down south in Denmark, Western Australia, my three children were old enough to have separate tents. In the middle of the night, the Dreamer raced into our tent and launched himself at me, wrapping his arms and legs around my body in a distressed and anxious manner. Shaken to the bone, I asked him what on earth had happened.

'I had a nightmare,' he whimpered.

'What was it about?' I asked.

'YOU!' he cried.

Parents, especially mothers, can unwittingly be both a source of comfort and trauma to their beloved children. But there's no one-size-fits-all theory, as everyone's a different size in this misshapen world of bittersweet relationships. Some personalities are more colourful than others, though.

While I can't cast the first stone at anyone from the Planet Thetan, or worse still, at another bad mother, there's quite a reasonable chance that a thrice-married poster child for Scientology would have had a mainly avoidant style of upbringing, while a head-shaven, limousine-bashing, rehab-shy pop princess may have had a mother who suffered from anxious attachment.

For me, consistent bonding didn't happen just because I gave birth. When my firstborn arrived, I'd already loved her in a deep and meaningful manner for nine months, but was so bewildered by the maternal process that I went into a state of shock.

Meanwhile, the rush of affinity with someone he'd help create had knocked my husband stupid, and he'd had a fierce loving connection with her the second she was born. It was three weeks before I felt that extrasensory blow to the brain. While I already would have killed anyone who'd come near her with harmful thoughts, the thunderbolt of bonding didn't hit me till 21 days later. When it finally did, it was so potent that the memory of it engraved itself onto my mind forever.

Attachment process is also what keeps me loving one son unconditionally even when he tells me he has an overwhelming urge to push me off the top of a cliff, and the reason why my other son hugs me tightly and kicks me in the shin at the same time. It explains why I look forward to my husband coming home from work, but five minutes after he has, I want to pick a fight with him about something that happened ten years ago. I would give up my life for my children, but snarl ferociously at them if they surreptitiously try to sneak bacon off my plate on a Sunday morning.

Luke Skywalker almost turned to the dark side of the force because of his attachment to his father. No matter how evil Darth Vader was (and, don't forget, he chopped off his only son's arm and never said sorry), the young, blonde freedom-fighter not only remained powerfully drawn to his paternal flesh and blood, he forgave him just before the Lord of Darkness died.

There are choices in this world. One of them is the ability to choose your friends and, to a lesser extent, civilised neighbours, work colleagues and casual acquaintances. But families are for life, for better or for worse; just as they don't arrive with a money-back guarantee, they always come with a strict no-return policy.

Motherhood 101

Sometimes my ponytail feels as if it's pulled too tightly off my face — and then I realise my hair is loose. Luckily, in the time between leaving home in my car and arriving at work, no-one except my John Denver CDs and expired rego sticker can hear me scream.

Working full-time and raising three teenagers doesn't make me Super Mum, it just makes me Super Tired and Super Bitchy. In the rush hour getting to work in order that I can take on my boss and my boss's boss, I have to take on the other great unwashed vehicles on the road as well. This is when I feel as though I've failed Good Mothering Skills 101 and passed Desperately Depressed Fishwives 404 with first-class honours.

It's easier to get Amy Winehouse into rehab than it is to get my kids clean, straight and sober for school. Not only do my boys lie straight in bed after the alarm clock's gone off fifteen times, they eyeball me, grin, and lie cheerfully through their grotty, yellow teeth that, yes, they have cleaned them properly. It's the camel breath that gives the game away.

They waste the equivalent of the water levels of the Canning Dam having their morning showers, from which they don't appear to emerge any cleaner than when they went in. We've had the same bar of soap in the shower for three years now — I don't think it's ever gotten wet.

An equal length of time is spent arguing over whose turn it is to feed the animals. Meanwhile, the dog's chomping the kitchen floor and the cats have dropped dead from starvation. But I wouldn't let my kids go hungry. Lunch for them is a Vegemite sandwich and an apple, and a stern lecture about childhood obesity and how in England I used to walk six miles barefoot in the snow to school.

Then, just when I have one, not-so-bare, foot out the front door, someone asks if I can write their teacher a note saying the dog ate their homework. And my reply is, thank God the dog has finally found something to eat. It's at this point I feel as though my whole face has been Botoxed by my tight ponytail and I feel like giving myself a Britney Spears buzzcut.

And when I start heading down the highway to work, it's all I can do NOT to turn the wheel in the direction of Perth International Airport. This is how I've learned that it's never, ever wise to carry one's passport in one's handbag.

Mother's way saves her day

What I want for Mother's Day isn't complicated. I just want my family to go out, enthusiastically sing silly songs in the car, and enjoy some quality time at a remote country location, my children helping their father burn snaggers and chops on the barbecue, and generally entertaining themselves joyously playing cricket and football. Enid Blyton, eat your heart out!

I, meanwhile, will stay at home, relaxing blissfully in a warm bath, surrounded by fragrant candles, fantasising about

Orlando Bloom and sipping a glass of chilled white wine, and NOT having my peace constantly shattered by people banging on the door wanting to know where their socks or jocks are.

Mother's Day should be a fantasy day on which I don't have to chisel my lazy children out of bed, then pick them up and plonk them under the shower, holding them under the water with one hand while the other does a frenzied search-and-rescue mission for dirty discarded school uniforms.

The next thing I wouldn't be doing is force-feeding health-department-approved breakfast cereal between gritted teeth (mine). I then wouldn't be cleaning the dishes with one hand, and holding the kids down and scrubbing the yellow gunge off their teeth with the other, before downing a lukewarm cup of coffee and heading out the door to face, yet another, eight hours chained to the computer. (Being at work seems to be the easiest part of my day.)

The last time we went out for a barbecue at a remote country location, my children jeered my suggestions of a jolly game of cricket. They preferred to stay in the comfort of the car, frantically exercising their thumbs with expensive Game Boys, and texting their friends (and enemies).

It started to rain at around about the same time we ran out of barbecue gas. Our fat, pale, half-cooked sausages lay out in the drizzle, while we sat in the car, steaming up the windows arguing about whose fault the weather was. As do most family arguments, this one remained unresolved.

When the rain stopped, we managed to get the kids interested enough in a game of cricket to actually want to play, by promising an ice-cream and a bag of lollies each, if they displayed a certain amount of enthusiasm.

So, given a choice on Mother's Day between my family's Big Day Out or a bubble bath with Orlando Bloom, it's a no-brainer. Pass the tomato sauce, please.

On the cat walk

As we all know, cats are really little women in fur coats. We have two in our household, as well as two small, furry creatures with long whiskers and lashing tails.

Grooming is essential to our cats. Many happy hours are spent licking, preening and primping, and, in the process, shedding dark fur over cream couches with gay abandon.

They are rather like my teenage daughter, who regularly takes over my bathroom with her vast array of cosmetics, pimple creams and hair products, and spreads — like warm sunshine, or a fungal disease — mascara and foundation over my newly scrubbed vanity cabinet. I've had more success persuading our cats to scratch out their fur and fleas in the direction of our kitchen bin than I have getting my daughter to put her clothes in the laundry basket.

Like our cats, she feels a royal level of entitlement to be waited on hand and foot by lesser mortals, including being fed dainty and delicious delights on a regular basis. She also feels she has the right to sleep serenely all day, be awake and active at night, and torture small, defenceless rodents, otherwise known as her brothers.

When, in the middle of the night, I hear a scratching noise at the front door, I'm never sure whether it's my daughter coming home or one of the cats wanting to go out. Sometimes it's both.

Sometimes it happens several times a night. I could complain, but experience has taught me that I'd just be meowing into a maelstrom.

Cats, like teenage girls, seem to have little purpose in life except to lie in the sun, look sensational, be admired by indulgent others, get underfoot and deliberately trip up the person who continually stands by them.

Cats and teenage girls also like to cross the invisible boundary that separates home from the dangerous but tantalising underworld. It's easy to be seduced by temptation. Teenagers have succumbed to it over the years, just like the sailors who were drawn to the sweet singing of the mythological sirens of the ocean, which caused them to dash their ships onto the rocks.

Teenage girls hear only what they want to, which is rarely their mother's voice. It's impossible to listen to someone else when you're hell-bent on smashing into the brick walls of life.

My job, as I see it, is to provide my daughter with a crash helmet strong enough to withstand the impact, thus allowing her to live her nine lives to the fullest.

Commonsense isn't so common

Parenting requires a certain amount of commonsense. But commonsense isn't so common in our household. We're the type of family who decides to have a major clear-out two weeks after the annual bulk rubbish collection.

This led me to rid myself of all the parenting advice books I'd collected over the years. You know the ones: *Bring up Your Children My Way or They'll End up in Prison*, *If You Smack Your*

Children, They'll End up on Smack and *The Evils of Full-time Child Care for Under Twos*.

When you tout yourself as a paragon putting yourself high upon the peak of perfection, the only place to go is downhill, sliding so fast that you wear out the seat of your pants. Not that this stops me trying, on the odd occasion, to attain that lofty position.

According to the latest research into Paradoxical Parenting, children should show more respect for their elders when they're on public transport. My kids' public behaviour can be in direct contrast to their private performances, and I'm very proud of them when they respectfully give up their seats without having to be asked.

In fact, they go cross-eyed and dizzy as they rapidly scan the aisles for someone elderly, pregnant or disabled, so that they can fall over themselves offering up their seat in a courteous manner. And they get really affronted when these people tell them that, no thanks, they would prefer to stand. On one occasion, the SmartRider made it his personal mission to persuade a middle-aged gentleman that his bum needed the seat more than my son's did.

Chucking out my treasured, dog-eared parenting books and relying on basic instinct instead, is rather like throwing out all unhealthy foods, and filling the fridge with vitamin-filled fresh fruit and vegetables. A sea change in which commonsense prevails.

The members of my family all sport well-rounded tummies, and I came to the realisation that good-enough parenting involves me being responsible for my children's eating habits. Not the federal government or the school lunchbox police, but me. Mother of three and wife of one. What I put into the weekly shopping trolley is displayed for all and sundry to see on my family's collective hips. Whether I like it or not, I'm the centre of their universe, even when I explode from a supernova into a deep, black hole.

And a good start in burning off unwanted kilojoules is to get my elderly butt off my comfortable train seat and stand up. Well, I would. If only my kids would let me.

Mothers and daughters

My teenage daughter and I have a generally wonderful relationship, enhanced by the fact that although we live under the same roof, we only see each other for five minutes every other day. She works a regular evening shift and I work a regular day shift.

I thought that it was high time that, instead of being ships that pass in the hallway, Daughter and I got to know each other better. So, we've booked ourselves into a six-star hotel room for a night to indulge in 'The Girl Thing'.

For me, this means an afternoon of nurturing and pampering. Doing nothing more strenuous than lying on our backs, and having soothing aromatherapy oils massaged deeply into our tired muscles by someone with very strong rejuvenating hands who also looks remarkably like a muscle-rippling Hugh Jackman.

We'll then head back to our luxury room, to soak in a warm bubbling spa bath before getting frocked up in our finest jewellery and evening wear. We'll dine on sumptuous cuisine in a top-class restaurant before arriving, via a stretch limousine, at His Majesty's Theatre to enjoy front-row-centre seats on the first night of the latest award-winning, critically acclaimed stage play about horses that stars a naked Harry Potter.

Back at our hotel room, we'll spoil ourselves silly ordering expensive French champagne and chocolate-covered strawberries from room service, and laughing uproariously at anything and everything while plaiting each other's hair, and generally care and share while wearing false nails, silly pyjamas and lurid fluorescent slippers.

For my daughter, the ultimate 'getting spoiled rotten' mother–daughter bonding experience means donning unironed all-black t-shirt, jeans and steel-capped work boots, shining her eyebrow, tongue and lip piercings with a bit of spit and polish, and hoofing it across town to queue up with a long, snaking line of Emo kids to see *Saw III* or anything starring the 'Jackass' team.

Dining in fine style for my Wild Child apprentice chef means ordering a Whopper with extra bacon, extra cheese and extra transfat. Back at our room in whichever hotel we've chosen for the night, we'd tear open some Chateau Cardboard for an all-night boozing session, and play some drinking games that involve shouting, 'Skoll! Skoll!' very loudly until 4 am, or until hotel security staff knock on our door. We'd possibly smoke a couple of dodgy herbal cigarettes on the balcony, before passing out on the starched, pristine bed covers.

Either way, it's going to be a night to remember.

Guilt for guilt's sake

Guilt, as defined by my dictionary, is 'Having committed an offence or feeling to blame for something'.

What! You mean like having given birth and wanting a life? That sort of thing? If so, I'm guilty as charged of:

HOUSEWORK GUILT

Because I'm supposed to, but don't, enjoy such wifely and motherly pastimes as ironing sheets and hankies, sterilising and pasteurising the floors and walls of my house, and baking bran and cardboard muffins, so the rest of my family can have healthy, interesting and fulfilling lives.

FEEDING-THE-FAMILY GUILT

Back in caveman days, life was much easier. Children either ate nuts and berries and woolly mammoths or starved. Simple!

GENERALISED MOTHER GUILT

This is the rich motherlode of shame for those working mums who get daily phone calls because:

- A) Little Johnny hasn't handed his homework in;
- B) Isn't wearing the correct uniform;
- C) Ate transfats for lunch; or
- D) All of the above.

FAT GUILT

This is what I felt when my body grew to a size 16 but my subsequent guilt bloated out to a size 28. It's also the pleasure I get when I eat at fast-food outlets so that I can ingest a thousand guilt-inducing kilojoules of lip-smacking grease, salt and preservatives wrapped up in a healthy bread bun.

ECO GUILT

This is the guilt I can't be bothered feeling when I toss potato peelings, plastic bags, empty soup cans and small children into the rubbish bin without first sorting them into general, polypropylene and other recyclable items.

CLOSET SMOKER'S GUILT

Remember the good old days when you could smoke yourself into a fug between the entrée and main course? Or lie in a hospital annexe kippering your lungs next to the oxygen tank? I still enjoy smoking. Only now it's guilt, rather than black tar, that sears my lungs.

GIN AND GALLIANO GUILT

Yet another allegedly legal substance taken to alleviate that stomach-clenching fear of having failed as a mother yet again. Sometimes enjoying a non-alcoholic lunch with family is a bit like having major surgery without general anaesthetic. Gin is not called 'mother's little helper' for no good reason.

GUILT FOR FEELING GUILTY

This is the guilt I feel for feeling guilty about a crime I haven't committed but feel responsible for anyway.

FATHER GUILT

A guilt-filled father is like the Loch Ness Monster or a tradesman that appears on time — a mythical creature that simply doesn't exit.

Curved learning

- ☑ I've learned that the older I get, the less I know. The less I know, the less I worry about, and the less I worry about, the happier I am. If I was happy this year, next year is going to be even more blissful.
- ☑ I've also learned this year that if you're going to spend a small fortune on environmentally friendly cloth shopping

bags, you should remember to take them into the shopping centre with you. They're not doing the earth much good stuck in the car.

- ☑ I've learned that when I come home from work and my daughter has tidied up her bedroom, swept the back verandah of all cigarette butts and beer cans, put flowers in the vase on the dining table, is cooking an elaborate five-course dinner, and pours me a glass of wine and tells me, 'That's the good news — now, here's the bad news,' that it probably involves yet another body piercing.
- ☑ I've learned that pierced-eyebrow — and — tongue teenage girls still love their parents and want to spend time with them.
- ☑ That meditation and quiet self-reflection, like sex and fresh air, is not only free, it's also one of the best things there is.
- ☑ That bananas at $35.99 a kilo can still be left uneaten to turn a mushy brown and end up getting thrown in the rubbish bin.
- ☑ That it's OK, even obligatory at some stage, to ignore the family and all other commitments in order to read *The Da Vinci Code* over a long weekend.
- ☑ That just because my children cannot pass each other in the hallway without resorting to fisticuffs, this doesn't mean they won't come to the party when their brother or sister is getting beaten up by the neighbourhood thug.
- ☑ That getting rid of all candles, matches, cigarette lighters and aerosol cans is the way to give one peace of mind when both parents work full-time and so have to leave two boys to their own devices during the Christmas school holidays.
- ☑ That if you open a packet of biscuits at the end where it says 'Open other end', the earth will not explode.

- ☑ That it's OK for everyone to eat corn flakes for dinner because I'm too tired to cook.
- ☑ I've learned that red wine goes with absolutely everything. Including breakfast cereal.
- ☑ And above all else that successful balance in life can be achieved with a self-help book in one hand and a glass of red wine in the other.

Acknowledgements

I would like to give many heartfelt thanks and praise to my husband of 22 years, Dave, whom our three teenagers willingly acknowledge has most excellent parenting skills, but will only say this behind closed doors. Somehow, between us, we've managed to bring up three surprisingly well-balanced adolescents.

To my three teenagers, Melissa, the Wild Child (18), Matthew, the Dreamer (15) and Christopher, the SmartRider (13) and all their mates who have crashed out on the family-room couches over the years. Thank you for providing me with many 'entertaining moments' and material for my writings. Someone close to my heart once told me to 'always talk (and listen) to your teenagers as if the person you once knew was still there'. Wise advice which has worked wonders.

I would like to give huge congratulations to my parents for getting divorced and remaining good friends. My mum is now very happy with her new husband John and his four adult children, Justin, Gareth, Emily and Felicity. My dad is ecstatic with his partner, Elaine, her poodles and her two daughters

Serena and Shauna. I now have more extended family to call upon than the Sopranos.

Many thanks to my darling sister Sarah and her fiancé, Jovan, and his three children Dejan, Milos and Jovana, plus their new baby. Sarah recently gave birth to the most beautiful baby in the world, my niece Angelia Anne. Not that I'm biased or anything.

And much love to my husband David's parents, Pat and Trevor, my in-laws — you know how much you mean to us all.

And thanks to:

Stephanie Calman, the one and only original Bad Mother Superior (www.badmothersclub.co.uk) who introduced me to the fine art of Bad Mothering in order to bring up healthy, happy and for the most part, well-adjusted children (and parents).

Rosemary Greenham, senior producer, ABC Radio 720, Perth, for all her support and encouragement over the years I have known her; she still manages to find time to be a Bad Mother in her very busy day. The first time I met her she told me one of her daughters had sent her an email warning she'd had yet another body part pierced. Oh, how I could relate to that!

Earl Reeve, for helping me with voice coaching and although I didn't quite get the posh BBC accent I desired, we did manage to produce something very unique for ABC 720 radio. It was a most enjoyable experience from someone truly wonderful and dedicated.

Sarah Knight and Bernadette Young, ABC Radio 720 Perth, for all your help, support and humourous off-air anecdotes over the four years my stories were broadcast.

Jo Mackay and Helen Littleton (themselves Bad Mothers) of ABC Books, the publishers and editors of both my books who have made many a great suggestion which has enhanced the quality of my writing. I thank you both for having faith in me.

Audrey Robertson in Manchester England for emailing me the address of the original Bad Mothers Club website back in 2003, which kick-started my writing career. And an even bigger thanks for her long, philosophical, hilarious emails about her two teenage boys which have had me in stitches over the many years we have been email buddies.

Thanks to all our very long-term friends with whom we've enjoyed many BBQ's and tears _ Jeanette and Peter, MaryAnne, Paul and Mayette, Maria and Tony, Helen, Christine and Tony and Doreen. We've all watched each others children grow up over the years into stunningly beautiful teenagers, both inside and out.

Gerry, Jude, Aylee and Krysia, my Churchill Clinic friends, with whom I can truly relax and be myself.

Jeanette, my childhood friend and website designer extraordinaire, who was one of the first people to use an internet chat room to contact, fall in love with, meet and marry an American and moved to Oklahoma in 1998. Her dogs are her teenagers.

Sharon Flynn, we met through the Bay City Rollers, but our friendship didn't end there. We've shared many a poignant Bad Mothers' moment with each other over the years.

Kathryn, a very Bad Mother of two beautiful girls, who is wicked fun over a takeaway curry and a bottle of wine or four.

Yvonne, my childhood schoolfriend who I sometimes don't see for many years but when we meet it's like we were never apart.

And last but never least, Jenny, my therapist, mentor, life-coach and friend (www.jenniferonline.com.au) — someone extraordinary who embraces life to the fullest and lives what she teaches. Her belief in the inherent goodness of all people has never wavered in the long time my family has known her.